# SHORT CUTS

INTRODUCTIONS TO FILM STUDIES

# SUBURBAN FANTASTIC CINEMA

## GROWING UP IN THE LATE TWENTIETH CENTURY

### ANGUS McFADZEAN

**WALLFLOWER**

LONDON and NEW YORK

A Wallflower Press book
Published by
Columbia University Press
Publishers Since 1893
New York • Chichester, West Sussex
cup.columbia.edu

Wallflower Press® is a registered trademark of Columbia University Press

Cataloging-in-Publication Data is available from the Library of Congress

ISBN 978-0-231-18995-8 (pbk.)
ISBN 978-0-231-54863-2 (e-book)

Book and cover design: Rob Bowden Design
Cover image: *E.T. The Extra Terrestrial* (1982) © Universal Pictures

# CONTENTS

## ACKNOWLEDGEMENTS

I would like to thank the Editorial Director of Wallflower Press, Yoram Allon, for accepting the book proposal and guiding it through to publication. Thanks also to all the team at Wallflower Press and the manuscript readers for the smooth journey to publication.

I would also like to thank Mark Bould, Sherryl Vint and Gerry Canavan for publishing the original article that inspired this book in *Science Fiction Film and Television* at Liverpool University Press.

I would have never been able to complete this book without the support of my partner Rachel and my family.

# INTRODUCTION

'Suburban fantastic cinema' is a name that designates a set of Hollywood movies that started to appear in the 1980s, in which pre-teen and teenage boys living within the suburbs are called upon to confront a disruptive fantastic force – ghosts, aliens, vampires, gremlins and malevolent robots. These films emerged out of adult-focused, suburban-set melodramas, children's fantasy stories, and old-fashioned sf, horror, fantasy and adventure films and television mainly of the 1950s, and became synonymous with the work of Steven Spielberg, Joe Dante, Robert Zemeckis and Chris Columbus. Typically marketed as children's films or 'family' films, they were key parts of the childhood of late-Generation Xer's and millennials. Indeed, suburban fantastic movies have been some of the top box-office performers of the last forty years. This suggests that they are not only well-made films in their own right, but that they are also tapping into something important within Western culture generally over the last forty years.

This book is the first attempt to bring this set of films together for critical scrutiny. It will explore the history of suburban fantastic cinema and develop a theory about these films. They will be defined by the synchronisation of a pre-teen or teenager's personal dilemmas with the intrusion of a fantastic event. The protagonist's melodrama develops in parallel with the crisis of the fantastic, and when the fantastic crisis is resolved, the protagonist's melodrama is also resolved. On one level, this synchronisation permits a narrative of maturation. The protagonist is maladjusted to their world and the fantastic brings to crisis this maladjustment as part of a process of growing up. The protagonist learns the value of loyalty, duty, honour, friendship, love and courage. All of their contradictions are resolved with a feeling of magical wonder. However, this synchronisation also permits a narrative of socialisation. By looking closely at suburban fantastic films, we can see that they depict a symbolic moment in which a child is socialised into the dominant ideologies of society. The protagonist's adventure fundamentally transforms their personality towards internalising a new set of values, which can be summarised as those of patriarchy. They are co-opted by a society of media manipulation, male domination and the rule of multinational capital. And at its most extreme, suburban fantastic cinema showcases a process of magical grooming, in which pre-teens reconcile themselves with even the most troublesome aspects of their society, in exchange for the positive heroic identity that will be validated by society.

This theory will be preceded by a survey of the historical development of the suburban fantastic. Chapter 1 will describe the historical origins of the suburban fantastic in the child-focused fantasy film, the small-town 'family film', and sf, horror and fantasy tropes from film and television. *Poltergeist* (Tobe Hooper, 1982) and *E.T.: The Extra-Terrestrial* (Steven Spielberg, 1982) were among the first to recognise and exploit the new pre-teen audience and offer representations of the kind of suburban landscape in which they were growing up, as well as representations of the kind of fantasies that were common to the suburbs. The first cycle of Amblin pictures, up to *Back to the Future* (Robert Zemeckis, 1985), developed a set of semantic and syntactic traits that other producers went on to develop.

Chapter 2 reviews the history of Hollywood, Amblin and independent productions over the last twenty-five years. Drawing on Rick Altman's theory of genrification, it identifies some of the major trends of suburban fantastic cinema – its extension into stories with teen and adult protagonists, its use as a subordinate element within a generic mix, and its relationship to other generic developments, such as blockbuster cinema, suburban satires and family films.

Chapters 3–5 move on to elaborate a theory of the suburban fantastic through a number of different perspectives. The main area of focus is the meaning of the element of the fantastic that intrudes into the protagonists' lives.

Chapter 3 explores how male identity crises are reflected in the element of the fantastic. Although the appearance of the fantastic joyfully resolves the contradictions in the protagonist's personal life, it also accelerates the protagonist's socialisation. Their heroism is established at the cost of an implicit compromise with the patriarchal order. This chapter explores this idea by showing how suburban fantastic cinema focuses on male characters at the expense of female characters, lower class characters and outcasts. Male identity is shown to be torn between the image of the young boy as a robotic weapon that can bring great destruction and the contrasting image of the young boy as a heroic Superman who can save everyone.

Chapter 4 traces the connection between the element of the fantastic and televisual and cinematic images that burst through the screen into the real world. It identifies the different attitudes suburban fantastic cinema has towards television and cinematic images and connects them to a wider privileging of technology and science in these films.

Chapter 5 identifies multinational capital as an invisible force that produces the element of the fantastic disrupting suburbia. This takes the form of government, military and scientific forces, which are often implicated in the appearance of the fantastic. We look at stories that make suburbia appear irredeemably corporate and contrast them with stories where suburbia and the fantastic are naturalised. We also consider the representation of suburban property developers and explain the symbolic importance of suburbia within suburban fantastic cinema.

Through Chapters 3–5 we consider some of the key examples of suburban fantastic cinema (*Explorers* (Joe Dante, 1985), *The Monster Squad* (Fred Dekker, 1987), *Matinee* (Joe Dante, 1993) and *Jumanji* (Joe Johnston, 1995)) in order to explore variations of this sub-genre. Finally, Chapter 6 considers the most recent development in suburban fantastic cinema, a loosening of the relationship between the protagonist and the element of the fantastic. This is apparent in Hollywood productions, as well as in self-conscious pastiches of the suburban fantastic that are here called 'reflexive' suburban fantastic films. *Super 8* (J.J. Abrams, 2011), *Stranger Things* (TV, 2016–) and *IT* (Andy Muschietti, 2017) are reviewed for the way that they consciously reference the history of the suburban fantastic, at the same time as adapting the sub-genre in response to new social, political, and technological realities and audience demographics. Indeed, it is through the emergence of these self-conscious suburban fantastic films that it has become possible to see the suburban fantastic sub-genre clearly for the first time.

# 1     EARLY SPIELBERG AND AMBLIN PRODUCTIONS, 1981–85

*Sources of the Suburban Fantastic*

Suburban fantastic cinema draws on three pre-established narrative tradi-tions: the child-focused fantasy film; the small-town 'family film'; and sf, horror and fantasy tropes from film and television.

*Child-Focused Fantasy Films*

As Noel Brown has highlighted, child-focused films that drew on a liter-ary tradition of children's adventure thrived in the age of sound: *Treasure Island* (Victor Fleming, 1934), *David Copperfield* (Clarence Brown, 1935), *Little Lord Fauntleroy* (John Cromwell, 1936), *Poor Little Rich Girl* (Irving Cummings, 1936), *The Adventures of Tom Sawyer* (Norman Taurog, 1938) and *The Little Princess* (Walter Lang, 1939) to name a few. However, it was the eventual success of *The Wizard of Oz* (Victor Fleming, 1939) that established the popularity of child-focused *fantasy*. Indeed, Dorothy's discontent at home, her journey to the magical world of Oz, and her rec-onciliation to her home-life, offers a proto-suburban fantastic narrative. Although it took some time for *The Wizard of Oz* to become a popular classic (through the 1948–9 re-release and its broadcast on television in the 1950s), it 'has come to be seen as the quintessential family film of the classical Hollywood cinema' (Brown 2017:42). Disney animated films such as *Pinocchio* (Ben Sharpsteen, Hamilton Luske, 1940), *Alice in Wonderland* (Clyde Geronimi, Wilfred Jackson, Hamilton Luske, 1951) and *Peter Pan* (Clyde Geronimi, Wilfred Jackson, Hamilton Luske, 1953) also drew upon the literary tradition of children's fantasy and perpetuated the success of child-focused fantasy.

However, despite the popularity of *The Wizard of Oz* and early Disney, child-focused fantasy itself was not strong enough to constitute a cycle of films, nor did fantasy constitute a viable box office genre. In the 1940s and 50s, children's fantasy edged into horror, science fiction and stronger forms of fantasy intermittently (Disney's first live-action movie *So Dear to My Heart* (Harold D. Schuster and Hamilton Luske, 1948), *The 5,000 Fingers of Dr. T.* (Roy Rowland, 1953), *The Invisible Boy* (Hermann Hoffman, 1957)) without significantly affecting its generic profile. In the 1960s a new kind of child-focused fantasy cycle emerged, harkening back to the musical *The Wizard of Oz* and Disney animations. *Mary Poppins* (Robert Stevenson, 1964), *Chitty Chitty Bang Bang* (Ken Hughes, UK, 1968), *Willy Wonka and the Chocolate Factory* (Mel Stuart, 1971) and *Bedknobs and Broomsticks* (Robert Stevenson, 1971) represent stereotypical bourgeois children living in idealised Victorian/Edwardian settings whose normal lives are disrupted by the intrusion – actual or imaginative – of an element of fantasy or science, commonly witches, wizards and inventors who lead them into surreal magical adventures. Although these child-focused fantasy films feature magical *technology* in places (the creation of a flying car, Willy Wonka's factory), they generally avoid sf in favour of magic. And usually the children return to their hometown at the end, having matured along the way and resolved their personal melodramas. These films therefore synchronise the children's desires and dilemmas with the fantastic events of their lives and constitute important precursors to the suburban fantastic.

Child-focused fantasy found a home in dedicated children's television as it emerged in the 1960s with *Lost in Space* (TV, 1965–8) and shows by Sid and Marty Krofft such as *Sigmund and the Sea-Monsters* (TV, 1973–5) and *The Lost Saucer* (TV, 1975–6). And Disney anticipated the advent of a child-focused fantastic in *Escape to Witch Mountain* (John Hough, 1975) and its sequel, *Return from Witch Mountain* (John Hough, 1978), which fused children's adventure with science-fiction. But until the advent of the suburban fantastic with *Poltergeist*, sf and horror were almost entirely absent from child-focused fantasy films.

## Small-town Family Films

Representations of families in small towns and an emerging suburbia have been a focus of cinema since the beginning of the sound era. As Noel Brown explains, '*Ah, Wilderness!* [Clarence Brown, 1935] was a template for a succession of long-running, cheaply-made family series spanning the late 1930s and early 1940s' (Brown 2012: 52), series such as Fox's comedies on the Jones family (1936–40), MGM's Hardy family comedies (1937–46) with Mickey Rooney, Republic Pictures' Higgins family (1939–41), and others. These were in some ways precursors to the family sitcoms of the 1950s, such as *Father Knows Best* (TV, 1954–60) and *Leave it to Beaver* (TV, 1957–63), a suburban-set sitcom that focused on the antics of pre-teen children.

In the 1940s, a cycle of prestige pictures focused on the 'nuclear' or 'extended' family and exhibited a notable romanticising, nostalgic attitude towards small-town life. These looked back from the 1940s to the turn of the twentieth century which was depicted as an idyllic time, 'a period of relative social stability, before widespread industrialisation, global warfare and economic depression' (Brown 2012: 81). Anticipated by *Our Town* (Sam Wood, 1940) and established by the success of *Meet Me in St Louis* (Vincent Minnelli, 1944), this cycle included *National Velvet* (Clarence Brown, 1945) and *The Yearling* (Clarence Brown, 1946) and was exemplified by *It's a Wonderful Life* (Frank Capra, 1946). Their representations of small towns were heavily sentimentalised and this nostalgic tone was inherited by suburban fantastic cinema of the 1980s.

*It's a Wonderful Life* is particularly important for the development of the suburban fantastic in that it shows a small town on the cusp of major suburban development and the main character's personal dramas are linked to the future development of the town. Indeed, through the 1940s onwards, the depiction of the small-town becomes conflated with the emergence of new suburbs. As Kenneth MacKinnon states, 'movies set in the suburbs of cities deliberately take on the look, and therefore share the charisma, of the small town movie' (MacKinnon 1984: 24). However, cinema's attitude to suburbia was quite different from its attitude to small-town America. As Brown states, 'the avowed self-sufficiency of suburban living precludes the community-orientation regarded as the bedrock of the small-town lifestyle' (Brown 2012: 92). Suburbia was seen negatively and this affected the representation of small towns as well. Stephen Rowley highlights the more acerbic vision of suburbia in *The Man in the Gray Flannel Suit* (Nunnally Johnson, 1956), *No Down Payment* (Martin Ritt, 1957) and *Bachelor in Paradise* (Jack Arnold, 1961) (Rowley 2015: 89–109); the ironic vision of typical American towns and families in Douglas Sirk's melodramas; and the effect of social changes in America through the 1960s in films like *The Graduate* (Mick Nichols, 1967) and *The Swimmer* (Frank Perry, 1968) (Rowley passim). Emanuel Levy summarised the change when he says that 'the tone of the movies changed, from light satire in the early 1950s to criticism in the late 1950s, to outright scorn, ridicule, and condemnation in the 1960s and 1970s' (Levy, 1991: 110). These critical representations of suburbia established what Bernice M. Murphy calls the 'suburban gothic', 'a sub-genre concerned [...] with playing upon the lingering suspicion that even the most ordinary-looking neighbourhood, or house, or family, has something to hide, and that no matter how calm and settled a place looks, it is only ever a moment away from dramatic (and generally sinister) incident' (Murphy 2009: 3). Murphy's idea of the suburban gothic establishes a fundamental split in the character of suburbia. Suburbia is the scene of domestic quarrels, adultery, divorce, alcoholism and unhappiness, but on the surface it appears as the utopian embodiment of the American Dream – safe, comfortable and homogenous. Since the establishment of suburbia in post-war America, this double character has become well-worn cliché. Suburban satires, such as *The Stepford Wives* (Bryan Forbes, 1975), mocked suburban social conformity and ennui. But although *The Stepford Wives* criticised the suburban way of life through a rare use of the fantastic (robot wives), small town and suburban set family films generally eschewed fantasy, notwithstanding the fantasy elements of *The Wizard of Oz* and *It's a Wonderful Life*.

*SF, Fantasy and Horror Film and Television*

In the absence of child-focused sf and horror, *adult*-focused narratives in fantasy, sf and horror met pre-teen viewers' demands for exciting spectacle. Hollywood offered to child viewers a sequence of sf and horror cycles, from Universal's horror cycle of the 1930s, to sf and horror B-movies of the 1950s, such as *The Beast from 20,000 Fathoms* (Eugene Lourie, 1953), *The War of the Worlds* (Byron Haskin, 1953), *It Came From Outer Space* (Jack Arnold, 1953), *This Island Earth* (Joseph M. Newman and Jack Arnold, 1955) and, most famously, *Invasion of the Body Snatchers* (Don Siegel, 1956). Although these films generally don't feature children as protagonists (cf. *Invaders from Mars* (William Cameron Menzies, 1953)), they were devoured by young viewers. Furthermore, the small-town settings of many sf and horror B-movies of the 1950s established the American small town as a space in which fantastic events can happen, a perception supported by science fiction and horror anthology TV shows like *Science Fiction Theater* (TV, 1955–7), *The Twilight Zone* (TV, 1959–64, 1985–9), *The Outer Limits* (TV, 1963–5) and *Night Gallery* (TV, 1970–3). They offered a repertoire of sf, horror and fantasy tropes, including aliens, vampires, monsters, and ghosts that went on to inspire the fantastic element of suburban fantastic cinema. Nevertheless, fantasy itself continued to be an awkward genre, having been partly absorbed into sf and horror, and otherwise disavowed as a viable, popular genre. Noel Brown talks of 'the North American public's apparent revulsion to overly escapist (i.e. "childish") or fantastic productions' and their 'preference in small towns for homely, earthy stories' (Brown 2012: 75), as if there was an implicit opposition between the two.

Things began to change when a new movie rating system was introduced in 1968. Horror underwent a resurgence through box office successes like *Rosemary's Baby* (Roman Polanski, 1968), *The Exorcist* (William Friedkin, 1973) and *The Omen* (Richard Donner, 1976). These films married an auteur style to exploitative material and lent new prestige to what was considered a pulpy genre. Furthermore, the looser ratings allowed for even more violent pulp horror to be released, as evidenced by the scandalous success of *The Texas Chain Saw Massacre* (Tobe Hooper, 1974). Spielberg played a part in this through the enormous box-office success of *Jaws* (Steven Spielberg, 1975), arguably an update of a 1950s-style monster movie. The intensity of these new adult horror films paradoxically established the ground for the emergence of more intense sf and fantasy films in the late 1970s.

This revival began when George Lucas and Steven Spielberg began to pastiche 40s pulp serials by Universal (*Buck Rogers*, *Flash Gordon*) and Republic (*Zorro*) that they and their audience had experienced as children. Lucas had anticipated the nostalgia for older cultural forms in his 60s-set *American Graffiti* (George Lucas, 1973) but it was box-office triumph of *Star Wars* (George Lucas, 1977), followed by the Spielberg-Lucas collaboration *Raiders of the Lost Ark* (Steven Spielberg, 1981) that firmly established this trend. The success of these productions was partly due to the fact that they unified 'family' and 'youth' audiences (Brown 2012: 154–5). Peter Krämer states that *Star Wars* was a 'turning point in American film history by moving family films, addressed to children and their parents as well as to the core cinema audience of teenagers and young adults, back to the centre of the American and global entertainment industry' (Krämer 2004: 366). These films refashioned the genres of space fantasy and historical adventure for an adult audience nostalgic for the entertainment they had experienced in their childhood, but also attracted a younger audience keen to experience the modern equivalent of the old adventure serials.

Some critics believed that the narratives of these and subsequent blockbuster films were simplified and became 'intellectually undemanding' (Wood 2003: 147). Famously, Robin Wood characterised this as 'Lucas-Spielberg Syndrome', 'catering to the desire for regression to infantilism, the doublethink phenomenon of pure fantasy' (2003: 155), 'films that construct the adult spectator as a child, or, more precisely, as a childish adult, an adult who would like to be a child' (2003: 145). These criticisms dogged the success of Lucas and Spielberg through the 1980s. Nevertheless, this combination of simplified story-telling, melodramatic conventions, special effects and nostalgia, proved a potent mix at the box-office. And the success of *Jaws*, *Star Wars* and *Raiders of the Lost Ark* set the stage for a new form of fantastic to consolidate itself: a blend of sf, horror, fantasy and adventure that, like *Jaws*, took place in the contemporary world, specifically in small-town America and its suburbs, but which was directed towards a younger audience.

## The Beginning of the Suburban Fantastic

Although Lucas and Spielberg had together revived sf and fantasy, Lucas never exhibits any interest in suburbia after *American Graffiti*. Indeed, Spielberg alone inaugurated the suburban fantastic, developing some of the key tropes that would appear in *Poltergeist* and *E.T.: The Extra-Terrestrial* in his 1977 film *Close Encounters of the Third Kind*, the first film of what both Andrew M. Gordon and James Kendrick have called Spielberg's 'suburban trilogy' (Gordon 2008: 55–8, 93–4; Kendrick 2014: 33–40). Generically, *Close Encounters* combines the 1950s small-town alien invasion movie with the 1970s paranoid conspiracy thriller and a spiritualised light-show, inspired by the climax of *2001: A Space Odyssey* (Stanley Kubrick, 1968).

The focus is on Roy Neary's (Richard Dreyfus) encounters with alien space-craft and his attempt to retrieve an image implanted in his mind by the aliens. The connection between Roy's personal family problems and the entrance of aliens into his life, the shots of suburbia at night-time, and his obsession with a mental image that appears in reality in the form of Devil's Tower in Wyoming, are all tropes that are developed by Spielberg in his subsequent projects.

In particular, Spielberg explores the suburban fantastic in scenes focusing on three-year-old Barry (Cary Guffey). Barry is introduced in a scene in which he is woken up in his bedroom by his electronic toys turn-ing on spontaneously, a scene manifesting the simple animistic belief of very young children who believe their toys are alive. The activity of the toys captivates Barry, but is also unnerving, especially when it is subsequently revealed as a by-product of the proximity of the aliens who later return and kidnap him. As James Kendrick notes, *Close Encounters* is 'the victim of an invasion by the horror genre':

> Although *Close Encounters* is a science fiction film, these scenes in the Guiler house are more aesthetically and tonally in line with horror films, particularly in the way their main effect is fear, rather than wonder, and it comes as little surprise that numerous ele-ments in these scenes are replayed with only minimal variation in *Poltergeist*. (Kendrick 2014: 58)

Barry journeys with the aliens throughout the rest of the film and he is hap-pily reunited with his mother at the end, after going on a fantastic adven-ture that has left him unharmed. But this journey takes place off-screen, behind the action focused on Roy's attempt to encounter the aliens again and Barry's mother's attempts to get him back.

Barry's situation and sensibility were brought to the fore when Spielberg developed 'Night Skies', an attempt to create a companion film to *Close Encounters*, focused on a more malevolent alien invasion. This science-fiction horror concept eventually resulted in two distinct but related films: *Poltergeist*, in which a ghost terrorises a family in a new suburban estate, and *E.T.: The Extra-Terrestrial*, in which a lonely suburban boy befriends an alien accidentally left behind by his race and protects him from apparently sinister government forces. It is with these films that the first suburban fantastic cycle was born. Together they organise a set of possible positions regarding the suburban fantastic. Where *Poltergeist* draws on horror, *E.T.* draws on science-fiction. Where *Poltergeist* is satirical of suburbia and its residents, *E.T.* is nostalgic and sentimental. Where *Poltergeist* was a studio production, involving a director-for-hire and Spielberg as producer, *E.T.* was a studio production involving a personal, semi-autobiographical story by Spielberg, who was director as well as producer. Joseph McBride quotes Spielberg as saying that 'One is about suburban evil, and the other is about suburban good' (McBride 2012: 336). Both, however, resolve the unbalanced sf/horror combination of 'Night Skies' by blending the genres of the suburban melodrama and the twentieth-century fantastic (science-fiction, horror and fantasy).

## Poltergeist

*Poltergeist* was released a week before *E.T.: The Extra-Terrestrial* in June 1982 and introduced a syntactical structure that came to define the suburban fantastic: the synchronisation of the characters' personal melodramas with the appearance of the fantastic element into suburbia. The protagonists are the parents, Diane (JoBeth Williams) and Steven Freeling (Craig T. Nelson) who are trying to cope with raising three children, all of whom have particular problems that worry them. The emergence of a disruptive ghost in their house through the TV set and the kidnapping of the youngest daughter, Carol Anne (Heather O'Rourke), manifests the parent's fears of child abduction and the dangers of modern technology. Meanwhile, the three children of the family suffer from various fears – clowns, a large tree outside the house, darkness – which are made manifest when a clown doll and the large tree come alive and the bedroom cupboard reveals a dark vortex to another dimension. The family's fight to save Carol-Anne brings them together and, despite its trauma, symbolically renews their bond to each other.

The split in *Poltergeist* between the personal melodramas of the adults and those of the children marks a transition from Bernice M. Murphy's suburban gothic to the suburban fantastic. While adult-centric suburban-set cinema experienced a revival in 1980s cinema and television through films such as *Ordinary People* (Robert Redford, 1980), *Blue Velvet* (David Lynch, 1986) and *Parenthood* (Ron Howard, 1989), representations of discontented suburban husbands and wives were now complimented by representations of anxious suburban children. This transition to a child-focused narrative is evident within *Poltergeist* and consolidated in *E.T.: The Extra-Terrestrial*. In these films, the melodrama is not manifested by revelations of personal betrayal or open interpersonal conflict but by the fantastical and imaginative appearance of children's emotional dilemmas.

Seen from a child's perspective, suburbia offers a differently doubled character to the suburban gothic. For children, suburbia is a self-contained, autonomous world, designed – with its schools, parks, skateparks, etc. – with the experience of childhood at its centre, a space in which children experience a degree of freedom and security. Establishing shots of the setting usually depict suburbia as a space of tranquil normality. The opening of *Poltergeist* shows the idyllic suburban estate of Cuesta Verde, where children cycle around on bikes, sit on the kerb playing with remote-control cars and buy ice-cream from a van. At the start of *Gremlins* (Joe Dante, 1984), Billy (Zach Gilligan) runs through the centre of town, calling out to people he knows, while children throw snowballs. And at the start of *Jumanji* and *Small Soldiers* (Joe Dante, 1998), the young heroes cycle around their small hometown, similarly calling out to other residents. Such establishing shots typify the harmony and community of suburban streets.

However, for children of a certain age, suburbia also manifests an uncanny aspect that is the product of their developmental stage and the topographical situation of suburbia. Suburbia is always separated from but adjacent to the larger adult world, which is only accessible through the exciting adult experience of driving a car and travelling to a larger urban environment where parents work. Pre-teens and teenagers are limited to the boundaries of their town in a way that adults aren't – hence the importance of the bicycle in the suburban fantastic as a symbol of their ability to travel freely across their 'realm'. The inevitability of growing-up and encountering the adult world lying beyond the suburban horizon is the source of anxiety to pre-teens and teenagers, and this anxiety is reflected in the plots of suburban fantastic movies, whereby the protagonists' dissatisfactory lives are disrupted by the appearance of an external force in their neighbourhood. Indeed, in *E.T.*, *Explorers*, *The 'burbs* (Joe Dante, 1989) and *The Iron Giant* (Brad Bird, 1999), the initial establishing shots of a peaceful suburbia are accompanied by shots of the night-sky or of space that gradually focus down into suburbia, thereby lending a cosmic

An everyday suburban street in *Poltergeist* (Tobe Hopper, 1982); Elliott on his bike in *E.T.: The Extra-Terrestrial* (Steven Spielberg, 1982).

and existential dimension to childhood anxieties about the world beyond suburbia.

The suburban gothic's defining split between a placid surface and a dark underbelly, then, is supplemented by the suburban fantastic's defining split between childish suburbia and the external adult world. Following Rick Altman's definitions of genres as hybrids of semantic-syntactic material, we can identify the suburban fantastic using two generic sets. Altman's semantic and syntactic model involves a combination of 'common traits, attitudes, characters, shots, locations, sets, and the like (the semantics)' with 'certain constitutive relationships between undesignated and variable placeholders (the syntax)' (Altman 1999: 218). The suburban fantastic inherits the semantic material of suburban culture (images of the suburban town, children cycling around the streets, the family dinner-table, the daily rhythms of suburban life) and the syntactic material of coming-of-age melodramas that underpin the interpersonal conflicts of small-town family films. Furthermore, it inherits and adapts the 'fantastic', meaning the semantic and syntactic material of other twentieth century fantastic genres (sf, horror, fantasy, action adventure) and redeploys them aligned with the protagonist's anxieties. The semantic material of the fantastic is the familiar list of monsters and occult technologies. The syntactic material tends to be a melodrama of the heroic male (see Gledhill 1987, Williams 1998). This involves protagonists who cannot directly express their emotions and so music, gesture, expressive *mise-en-scène*, and generally the spectacle of action (in this case, the spectacle of the fantastic) stands in for this mute emotion (see Brooks 1976). The successful conclusion of male action constitutes the 'victory' of male identity. These melodramas of 'triumphant action' are combined with the emotional melodramas of small-town family films. Suburban fantastic, then, is a space of overlap between two larger generic sets, the semantic and syntactic language of suburban-set melodramas with the semantic and syntactic language of the fantastic.

## E.T.: The Extra-Terrestrial

The suburban fantastic demonstrated in *Poltergeist* – suburban melodrama spliced with haunted house horror – was continued and developed in *E.T.* – where suburban melodrama is spliced with an sf first contact story. Where *Poltergeist* split the connection to the fantastic between the parents and the children, however, *E.T.: The Extra-Terrestrial* puts the children's point of view at the centre of its narrative and distances the parental perspective. At the beginning of the film, Elliott (Henry Thomas) is experiencing a personal crisis: his father has recently left the family and Elliott is struggling to accept this absence, feeling alienated from his family and lonely in school. When he encounters E.T., he decides to protect him from the government forces looking for him. E.T. and Elliott develop a telepathic connection that allows them to feel what the other is feeling. When Elliott cuts his finger, E.T. heals his wound with a touch. By successfully bringing E.T. to his spaceship so he can return home, Elliott symbolically resolves his feelings of loneliness, alienation and despair. The final image of the film offers a distinctive Spielbergian sense of wonder: Elliott's face, bathed in light, looking up at the departing spaceship, having resolved his personal melodramatic conflicts through his encounter with E.T.

*E.T.*'s child-focused suburban fantastic draws on suburban melodrama and 1950s alien visitor movies but it also has a precedent in the children's fantasy film tradition. Andrew M. Gordon, amongst others, highlights its echoes of *The Wizard of Oz* (Gordon 2008: 90). *The Guardian*'s Derek Malcolm called it 'the perfect Disney movie' (Malcolm 1982: 13). And Spielberg acknowledges these connections himself when Gerty and Mary (Dee Wallace) read *Peter Pan* together in the film. However, the suburban fantastic demonstrated in *E.T.* develops the narrative model of children's fantasy by adding a contemporary suburban setting derived from suburban melodrama, clarifying the reality of the element of the fantastic, and strengthening the *symbolic* connection between the interior consciousness of the protagonist and the external force that disrupts their reality. The appearance of E.T. in suburbia is a real and objective event *and simultaneously* a projection of Elliott's fears and anxieties about abandonment by his father. Indeed, the suburban fantastic never treats the appearance of these elements of the fantastic merely as wish-fulfilling dreams. The fact that Elliott is not merely experiencing private fantasies is affirmed by the fact that whenever he tries to tell his mother or siblings about E.T., he is accused of being over-imaginative, until they witness E.T. for themselves.

Mary: All we're trying to say is, maybe you just probably imagined it. It happened...
Elliott: I couldn't have imagined it!
Michael: Maybe it was a pervert or a deformed kid or something.
Gertie: A deformed kid.
Michael: [mockingly] Maybe an elf or a leprechaun.

The moment in which the protagonist insists the element of the fantastic is real, but is dismissed for indulging private fantasies, is common to many suburban fantastic films (cf. *Cloak and Dagger* (Richard Franklin, 1984), *Explorers, The Monster Squad, Small Soldiers, The Iron Giant*) and has its counterpart in a scene when the parents realise their child was telling the truth all along and apologise for not believing him. The verifiable reality of the element of the fantastic is important because it allows the emotional concerns of the protagonist to be taken seriously and not dismissed as merely irrelevant feeling. Indeed, the wonder and transcendence of E.T.'s final scene becomes an important identifier of suburban fantastic cinema.

The phenomenal critical and commercial success of *E.T.* (the biggest grossing film of all time until *Jurassic Park* (Steven Spielberg, 1993)) established the viability of this semantic/syntactic model. After *E.T.*, the synchronisation of pre-teen or teenage melodrama with a fantastic event became a defining characteristic of a number of successful films. It is possible that suburban fantastic cinema would have emerged without the catalyst of Spielberg's 'Night Skies' project. The scripts for *Gremlins* and *Back to the Future* were initiated without Spielberg's influence. Furthermore some early 1980s films – *The Watcher in the Woods* (John Hough, US/UK, 1980), *Time Bandits* (Terry Gilliam, UK, 1981), *Something Wicked This Way Comes* (Jack Clayton, 1983) – suggest an audience existed for a more intense form of children's fantasy. However, working as a producer for his company Amblin Entertainment through the 1980s and 1990s, Spielberg continued to be integral to a series of box-office successes that established a semantic and syntactic cycle of suburban set melodrama with a focus on pre-teen and teenage protagonists and elements of the fantastic. Through Spielberg and Amblin, suburban fantastic cinema could be a producer-led cinema, where Spielberg's name, foregrounded in a film's promotion, was an imprimatur to the audience for the tone and quality of the movie. Amblin's production logo of Elliott's flying bicycle, indicated the extent to which the productions of Amblin Entertainment would be following in the footsteps of *E.T.*

## Gremlins and Joe Dante

After *E.T.*, Spielberg produced a film adaptation of the popular long-running TV show *The Twilight Zone*. Co-directed with George Miller, Joe Dante and John Landis, *The Twilight Zone: The Movie* (1983) remains notable chiefly for the contribution from Joe Dante. Dante's *Piranha* (1978) was a pastiche of Spielberg's *Jaws* and his werewolf film *The Howling* (1981) starred Dee Wallace, who played Elliott's mother in *E.T.* His segment of *The Twilight Zone*, 'It's a Good Life', was explicitly in the vein of the suburban fantastic. It tells the story of a pre-teen who has watched too many cartoons and has the power to make his imagination become real for other people, with nightmarish results. These films revealed that Dante had a sensibility sympathetic to Spielberg's emerging new generic blend and led to him directing the Chris Columbus-scripted *Gremlins* for Amblin.

*Gremlins* also blended melodrama (this time, in a small town) with a pastiche of 1950s science-fiction/horror B-movies but it did so by combining the anarchic negativity of *Poltergeist* (the gleeful destruction of domestic interiors) with the heart-warming sentimentality of *E.T.* (centred on Christmas and the cute 'mogwai', Gizmo). The narrative of *Gremlins* – in which an invasion of monsters into a small town parallels a melodrama of male gender identity – features key aspects of the emerging suburban fantastic. The main characters have just left school, but are trapped in post-childhood limbo, being not quite yet independent adults. Billy (Zach Gilligan) suffers from a number of humiliations: his frustrated desire to become a cartoonist of fantastic creatures, his desire for Kate (Phoebe Cates) and his parents' concern about his immaturity and day-dreaming. His irresponsibility while looking after Gizmo causes a group of gremlins to spawn from Gizmo, an event that takes place on a table covered with Billy's cartoons of grotesque creatures, suggesting that they are also symbolically born of his frustrated imagination. The gremlins go on to wreak havoc on the town. However, Billy displays bravery in confronting them and saving the town. He is 'rewarded' with Kate as a girlfriend, but because of the chaos that is unleashed, he is ultimately judged not mature enough to keep Gizmo. The story ends with the hope that one day Billy will be able to look after Gizmo responsibly.

*Gremlins*, then, adheres largely to the semantic/syntactic mix set up by *E.T.* but it also makes some alterations that indicate future lines of development for the cycle. In addition to featuring young adult characters rather than pre-teens, *Gremlins* accentuates the pastiche aspect of the suburban fantastic. *Poltergeist* and *E.T.* are relatively 'straight' films, rather than being, as Richard Dyer calls pastiche, 'a kind of imitation that you are meant to know is an imitation' (Dyer 2007: 1). Yet both the small town setting and the imitation of 1950s sf/horror B-movies in *Gremlins* foreground a sense of pastiche. Film posters in Billy's bedroom of *Them!* (Gordon Douglas, 1954) and *Beginning of the End* (Bert I. Gordon, 1957) indicate that the invasion of the gremlins is a pastiche of older sf/horror stories. And a clip from *It's a Wonderful Life* explicitly connects the Christmas-

The town of Kingston Falls in *Gremlins* (Joe Dante, 1984), evoking Bedford Falls in *It's A Wonderful Life* (Frank Capra, 1946).

time small-town setting of Kingston Falls to the nostalgic vision of Capra's Bedford Falls. The inclusion of this particular reference also highlights the tendency of suburban fantastic films to pastiche iconography that was established in small-town family films and suburban melodramas of the 1940s. Just as *It's a Wonderful Life* and other small-town-set stories of the 1940s looked back to the small towns of the turn of the century, so too does the suburban fantastic of the 1980s look back to the 1940s and 50s small town from the perspective of forty years of post-war suburban development. *Gremlins* pastiches 1950s small town iconography (the white picket fence cliché), and the pop culture of the period (Christmas music and classical Hollywood movies). Indeed, we will see that suburban fantastic films commonly pastiche other representational forms and balance this with their own 'straight' melodrama.

*Gremlins* also involves meta-referential touches that helped to establish it as part of an emerging cycle of films. For example, in *Gremlins*, the local cinema is showing 'A Boy's Life' and 'Watch the Skies', two working titles used by Spielberg for *E.T.* and *Close Encounters* respectively ('Watch the skies' is also a line from *The Thing From Another World* (Christian Nyby, 1951), suggesting a further connection back to 50s sf horror). And during the climax, Stripe, the lead gremlin, hides amongst soft toys of familiar cartoon characters such as Sylvester the Cat, Bugs Bunny and also E.T., thereby evoking *E.T.* in general, but also a specific scene in *E.T.* where E.T. hides amongst Gerty's soft toys. These are not just homages to Spielberg, but acknowledgements of his films as precursors to *Gremlins*. Such references to previous suburban fantastic films become common to subsequent suburban fantastic films. For example, at one point in *Cloak and Dagger*, Henry Thomas, the boy-star of *E.T.*, stands before an image of E.T. on an Atari video-game poster. In *Poltergeist II: The Other Side* (Brian Gibson, 1986), Carol-Anne has a poster for *E.T.* in her bedroom that can be seen when she is first attacked by the ghost. And films such as *Making Contact* (a.k.a. *Joey*) (Roland Emmerich, 1985), and *Mac & Me* (Stewart Raffill, 1988) repeat motifs and scenes directly from *Poltergeist* and *E.T.* (the haunted cupboard, attracting the alien with sweets, the death and resurrection of the main character).

*Gremlins* was a big success and further testified to the box-office potential of the emerging suburban fantastic model. It also went on to inspire numerous other comedy-horror films about homoculi (*Ghoulies*

(Luca Bercovici, 1984), *Critters* (Stephen Herek, 1986), *Hobgoblins* (Rick Sloane, 1988)), and offered an important example of the sub-genre of comedy horror (see William Paul 1994), which came to prominence in parallel with suburban fantastic cinema. However it was also a source of controversy because of the level of violence in what was supposedly intended to be a film for kids. The ratings agency had also received criticism for passing *Poltergeist* as a PG, not an R, a decision that was influenced by the economic prospects of the film. And, as James Kendrick explains, it was *Gremlins* together with the Spielberg-directed *Indiana Jones and the Temple of Doom* (1984), a film marketed to children that was similarly criticized for its violence, that led Spielberg to advocate for the creation of a new rating that would reflect the content of films that were designed for pre-teens (Kendrick 2009: 170–203). This became the PG-13 rating and it institutionalised a new audience demographic that was ready to experience something more adult than traditional children's fare, but who were still excluded from R-rated entertainment. After its introduction in June 1984, filmmakers could tailor their films towards this new rating, and such movies were fundamental in shaping the emergence of the 'pre-teen' as a social identity and consumer demographic. Notably it now became acceptable, if controversial, to include mild swearing in what were ostensibly kid's films, to better reflect the language that this audience actually used.

Dante went on to exhibit a remarkable sympathy for the suburban fantastic over the course of his career. He directed *Innerspace* (1987) and *Small Soldiers* for Amblin, and for other studios also directed further variations on the suburban fantastic such as *Explorers*, *The 'burbs*, *Matinee* and *The Hole* (2009), while also directing and acting as creative consultant on the cult suburban fantastic TV series *Eerie, Indiana* (TV, 1991–2). Dante's interest in suburbia as a landscape of the imagination, in children as protagonists, and his explicit debt to horror and sf films of the 1950s, allowed him to develop a distinctive tonal mix of satirical comedy and horror, which offered other producers an example of a middle road between the extremes of *Poltergeist* and *E.T.* However, despite helping establish the original cycle of suburban fantastic films, Dante's contributions often subvert the ideological assumptions of suburban fantastic cinema. As his direct citations of Spielberg in *Gremlins* indicate, Dante is very aware of the conventions of these stories. His films help clarify the characteristics of this sub-genre, while also providing some of its most entertaining examples.

*The Goonies*

Within a year, *Gremlins* was followed by *The Goonies* (Richard Donner, 1985), also from a script from Chris Columbus, this time based on an idea by Spielberg. *The Goonies* downplays the iconography of suburbia and small towns in favour of a more naturalistic boondocks aesthetic, focuses on the melodrama of a pre-teen friendship group, and pastiches adventure cinema rather than sf. *Poltergeist, E.T.* and *Gremlins* all incorporate a sense of adventure within their sf and horror pastiches, but *The Goonies* brings its pastiche of adventure to the fore and combines it with touches of horror, sentimentality and a simultaneously realistic and cartoonish threat from a family of crooks.

Within these variations of the semantic material, the syntactic connection between the protagonists' dilemmas and the element of the fantastic remains clear. The story occurs on one of the kids' last days living in the area, since their family homes are going to be repossessed to make way for the expanding Country Club. Mikey (Sean Astin) discovers a newspaper clipping and pirate treasure map in his attic, so his group of pre-teen friends (as well as his teenage brother and his friends) journey into a series of underground caverns full of booby-traps, pursued by a family of crooks who are also after the treasure. By navigating the booby-traps and defeating the 'bad family' of the crooks, they claim enough of the treasure to save their family homes from being demolished. Like *E.T.* then, *The Goonies* highlights the wish-fulfilling, fairy tale quality of suburban fantastic films. Even as they become heroes and prove their friendship, they also 'pay back' their parents and avoid moving house, fantasies that are recognisable to many kids.

For a pre-teen audience, such 'fairy tale' happy endings can have a very positive influence on character formation and maturation. As Bruno Bettelheim explains, fairy tales address children's feelings of weakness and inadequacy and give them satisfying models for dealing with crises in which their powers are tested (Bettelheim 1976: 57–8). The conclusions of other suburban fantastic films are often similarly restorative and magical (cf. *Making Contact, SpaceCamp* (Harry Winer, 1986), *\*batteries not included* (Matthew Robbins, 1987)). However, the happy endings of suburban fantastic films are not purely the symbolic resolutions of irresolvable psychological contradictions. Jack Zipes explains that 'Fairy tales and children's literature were written with the purpose of socializing children to meet definite normative expectations at home and in the public sphere' (Zipes 2012: 9). According to Zipes, children are indoctrinated by fairy tales into conventional manners and mores that reflect the social power, prestige and hierarchy of the ruling classes. The fairy tale resolution of *The Goonies* indicates that the protagonists of suburban fantastic are not undergoing a purely natural process of maturation but are being socialised through a particular fantastic trial into a set of values that are meant to be taken for granted. In the case of *The Goonies*, the characters develop an adult maturity through their adventure, but only with the purpose of postponing adulthood entirely and remaining children in their family homes for a bit longer. The children resolve the threat to their way of life by magically obtaining jewels that allow their home lives to continue as they are. When critics like Robin Wood have lamented the degree to which myth and fairy tale have underpinned these productions, it is this process of ideological conditioning that has concerned them. We shall see that this process of socialisation is an important part of suburban fantastic cinema.

*Back to the Future*

Only a month after *The Goonies*'s box-office success, *Back to the Future* was released. Written by Bob Gale and Robert Zemeckis, and directed by Zemeckis, it became the number one box office hit of 1985, spawning back-to-back sequels in 1989 and 1990. *Back to the Future* combines Marty McFly's (Michael J. Fox) suburban/small town melodrama (involving his school, his family, his musical ambitions and his desire for a car) with a science fiction narrative in which he accidentally time-travels back to 1955. Marty's main issue is that he feels alienated from his unsuccessful parents in 1985. The element of the fantastic (a time-travelling DeLorean) that disrupts Marty's suburban life allows him to encounter his parents in 1955 when they were his age. Marty interrupts a key encounter between his weedy nerd father George McFly (Crispin Glover) and his future mother Lorraine (Lea Thompson), and so has to help his father defeat the local bully and win the affection of Lorraine. Marty's time with his parents gives him a greater appreciation of them; it also resolves his musical ambitions when he anachronistically plays a rock'n'roll song and inspires Chuck Berry's musical sound. When he gets back to his own time, he discovers

*Back to the Future* (Robert Zemeckis, 1985) compares the promise of the suburbs in the 1950s to their faded reality in the 1980s.

that he has re-masculinised his father to such an extent that his family fortunes have improved dramatically. His major personal issues have also been resolved, a resolution capped by Marty getting a new car.

*Back to the Future*'s correlation of Marty's personal melodramas to an element of the fantastic (time-travel) is clear. However, the film also develops the representation of the fantastic in an interesting direction. By returning to the setting of the 1950s, *Back to the Future* goes further than the allusions to the 1950s in *Gremlins* and excavates the socio-political history that underpins the existence of the suburban fantastic as a semantic and syntactic blend. It was the suburban construction boom, the childhood of the baby-boomers, and the widespread introduction of television in the 1950s that provided the foundation of suburban culture in the 1980s and the semantic material for the suburban fantastic. By uncannily resurrecting the 1950s as a living reality, *Back to the Future* reveals that the element of the fantastic in suburban fantastic films is partly about the protagonist's anxious discovery of the socio-political roots of the present day. They are slowly discovering the real existence of a world before their birth, the world of their parents' adolescence, a world that created the conditions that allows their existence today, and they experience this discovery as a disturbing intrusion into their everyday lives.

Yet *Back to the Future* also poses questions about Marty's ability to access that past. Marty enters the past of 1955 through a time-travelling car, but the film's version of 1955 derives almost entirely from previous cinematic and cultural representations. Its dialogue reuses lines from *Rebel Without a Cause* (Nicholas Ray, 1955) and *A Streetcar Named Desire* (Elia Kazan, 1951). Its diegetic music includes pop songs typical of the time. And it pastiches 1950s melodrama in general in the contest between weedy George McFly and the bully Biff Tannen (Thomas F. Wilson). Vivian Sobchack goes further, arguing that 'in both the 1980s and the 1950s, Marty inhabits a nostalgically imagined, romantically generalized American small town' (Sobchack 1997: 274). Indeed, the town centre of Hill Valley in both periods was filmed on Universal's Courthouse Square set that had represented the town centre of Mayfield in *Leave it to Beaver* and was also used for *Gremlins* (Rowley 2015: 111–2). And the tension between the 'good town' of 1955 and the 'bad town' of 1985, dominated by rapacious capitalism, goes back to *It's A Wonderful Life* and the vision of Pottersville, a version of Bedford Falls that might have happened, had George Bailey (James Stewart) not been born.

Both the 1955 set and 1985 set portions of the film, then, form what Fredric Jameson calls a 'nostalgia film':

Nostalgia films restructure the whole issue of pastiche and project it onto a collective and social level, where the desperate attempt to appropriate a missing past is now refracted through the iron law of fashion change and the emergent ideology of the generation. (Jameson 1991: 19)

Such representations mobilise the iconography of a historical period without attempting an authentic reconstruction of the socio-political period; they transform images into visual commodities which are consumed by the viewer, and are symptoms of the resistance of contemporary raw material to artistic production (Jameson 1991: 16–25). *Back to the Future* suggests that the protagonist's encounter with the element of the fantastic can be a flawed attempt to stage an encounter between the suburban audience and their own suppressed history. Indeed, nostalgia and history become important factors in future suburban fantastic productions.

## The End of the First Amblin Cycle

After the back-to-back success for Amblin of *Gremlins*, *The Goonies* and *Back to the Future* (numbers four, six and one of the box office of their respective years), it was clear that there was enormous box-office potential for films that imitated the Amblin model: a syntactic connection between the protagonist and the element of the fantastic, and varying semantic elements such as a suburban setting, preteen children, an element of the fantastic and a mixture of Spielbergian wonder and terror. By the 1980s, mass suburbanisation had created a large new audience demographic of affluent, educated children who were ready to receive movies expressing the subjectivity and sensibility created by the shared generational and historical experience of suburban childhood. They had already been exposed through television to Hollywood films and this has offered underage viewers an early and premature entrance of adult reality. They were now ready to receive PG-13 suburban-set stories tailored to span the divide between children's family films and adult sf, horror and fantasy. And although these films were often pitched to male children and young teenagers, the distinctive Amblin mixture of emotionalism and terror was similarly appealing to young girls. Indeed, like *Star Wars* and *Indiana Jones*, these films could even be enjoyed by adults who could appreciate the allusions to sf, horror and fantasy films from their own childhoods.

This new audience of Hollywood cinema was catered to by a generation of Hollywood baby boomer writers and directors (Spielberg, Dante,

Columbus, Gale, Zemeckis) whose teenage years coincided with the first wave of suburbanisation and who had started to enter the Hollywood entertainment industry in the 1970s. They had grown up watching an older generation of sci-fi, horror and monster movies, and science fiction and horror anthology TV shows, media that disrupted the filmmakers' own dull suburban lives and inspired them with a passion for cinema. Now that they were entering Hollywood themselves, they took the opportunity to acknowledge the legacy of these experiences in their own work. Spielberg even revived the anthology format first with *The Twilight Zone: The Movie* and then with *Amazing Stories* (TV, 1985–7) and Dante arguably did the same with *Eerie, Indiana*. But suburban fantastic films are stronger testaments to the filmmakers' childhood love of the media that made them want to become directors in the first place. They affectionately pastiche their favourite genres, while also delivering to the audience excitement and thrills comparable to the effect of the original inspirations. And they add to those original inspirations a coming of age narrative, in which the protagonist's personal melodramas and TV-viewing experiences are connected to an element of the fantastic disrupting their suburban life. The filmmakers' inspiration in their childhood viewing, then, parallels the pre-teen characters' passion for sf and horror classics. And the resolution of the filmmakers' inspiration – in the production of suburban fantastic movies and the fulfilment of their desire to become directors – is reflected in the resolution of the pre-teen protagonists' coming of age into adult life.

That said, the creation of the suburban fantastic was not purely the product of auteurs like Spielberg, Dante and Zemeckis who wanted to represent something of their early movie passions and/or upbringing in suburbia in their movies. Production companies were interested in suburban fantastic films because, rather than being individualised coming of age stories (like, for example, Fellini's *Amarcord* (1973)), they drew upon pre-established Hollywood genres of melodrama and pastiche and so were available to being mass-produced as corporate products facilitating a historically specific market. The influence of market demographics on the suburban fantastic is indicated by the fact that most of these films are set in the present, rather than returning to the actual temporal location of the filmmakers' childhood. Nor do most of these films return to the precise area that might have inspired the filmmaker (John Hughes's preference for the Chicago suburbs is a notable exception). Instead, personal experiences were adapted into generic models and these formed the basis for further generic variation which lacked any overt personal input from the director.

By 1984, Amblin was beginning to face competition. Other studios and production companies were already creating their own instances of suburban fantastic cinema that radically expanded the possibilities of the model. Imagine Entertainment, Castle Rock Entertainment, and Touchstone Pictures all tried to capitalise on Amblin's success in family entertainment. The production of *The Karate Kid* (John G. Avildsen, 1984) and *Cloak and Dagger* (1984) indicated that the suburban fantastic was already diverging away from the fantastic towards genres like sports and adventure, and *Starman* (John Carpenter, 1984) indicated a shift from suburban pre-teens to adult romance. And many other hits of 1984 featured elements of the Amblin model – *The Last Starfighter* (Nick Castle, 1984), *Ghostbusters* (Ivan Reitman, 1984), *The Never Ending Story* (Wolfgang Petersen, 1984), *Red Dawn* (John Milius, 1984), *A Nightmare on Elm Street* (Wes Craven, 1984) – although none of these would be unambiguously categorised as suburban fantastic. Later, Amblin would successfully respond to non-Amblin productions, developing further variations on the basic suburban fantastic template, combining it with other genres and reweighing the tone from satire to sentiment, terror to Spielbergian wonder. But they were never again able to own the model as successfully as they did between 1982–5.

## 2    HOLLYWOOD AND INDEPENDENT PRODUCTIONS, 1983–1999

The success of the first Amblin cycle signalled the emergence of a commercially profitable semantic/syntactic blend and an audience that had learnt to recognise and enjoy its narratives. Unsurprisingly, other writers, directors, production companies and studios within and without the Hollywood system were interested in capitalising on Amblin's success by imitating and varying Amblin's most successful films. In doing so, they developed and standardised new codes of representation and new semantic and syntactic combinations, as part of the process of genrification. This was a collective and uncoordinated process, subject to the contingencies that affect all film productions. The films that resulted included ones in which a boy who fantasies about being a secret agent gets caught up in a real spy plot (*Cloak and Dagger*); a suburban boy is revealed to be an experimental super-robot that has escaped from the military (*D.A.R.Y.L.*, Simon Wincer, 1985); three boys build a space pod and travel to a nearby alien spaceship (*Explorers*); two boys use science to create their perfect woman (*Weird Science*, John Hughes, 1986); a boy is abducted by an alien that has escaped from NASA (*Flight of the Navigator*, Randal Kleiser, 1986); a group of children are called upon to fight off a collection of old Universal Studios monsters (*The Monster Squad*); a group of teenagers fight off vampires (*The Lost Boys*, Joel Schumacher, 1987); and three suburban fathers suspect their neighbour of being a murderer (*The 'burbs*).

In the 1990s, suburban fantastic films were heavily shaped by the resurgence 'family film', as defined by Noel Brown (Brown 2012: 4–13), which tamed some of the model's anarchy and adult terror. The films that resulted included those in which an inventor-father accidentally shrinks his own children who have to then survive a journey through their back-garden and house (*Honey, I Shrunk the Kids,* Joe Johnston, 1989); a boy accidentally releases a group of witches who create havoc on Halloween (*Hocus Pocus,* Kenny Ortega, 1993); a timid boy gets stuck in the pages of an adventure book (*The Pagemaster,* Joe Johnston and Maurice Hunt, 1994); an unhappy boy is trapped in a magical board game for twenty-six years and is forced to play it to return to his own time (*Jumanji*); and a lonely boy befriends a giant robot who is sought by the military (*The Iron Giant*).

In addition, Amblin continued to produce their own further iterations. *Harry and the Hendersons* (William Dear, 1987) imitates the Spielbergian wonder of *E.T.* but substitutes the connection between a young boy and a small alien with a grown father and a large sasquatch. The melodrama consequently focuses on the father's role in the family, rather than on the children. *\*batteries not included* substitutes the suburban setting and the pre-teen male protagonist for the working-class residents of a condemned city tenement, but the story of an alien race of friendly robots who build things and help them save the tenement from demolition shows many of the hallmarks of the suburban fantastic. *Arachnaphobia* (Frank Marshall, 1990) also focuses on adults and attempts to recreate the tone of 1950s horror films that inspire the suburban fantastic. *Casper* (Brad Silberling, 1995) focuses on the personal melodramas of a young girl and a ghost in the context of a haunted house story, exchanging the suburban set-ting for the gothic visuality inspired by the success of *The Addams Family* (Barry Sonnenfeld, 1991). Finally, *Small Soldiers* connects a suburban boy's behavioural issues to a new set of action figures that come alive and terrorise his hometown, complementing a traditional suburban fan-tastic narrative with a satire of war movies and modern corporate culture. Although these films had different degrees of involvement from Spielberg, they all involve reworking the semantic/syntactic blend that made *E.T.* and *Poltergeist* so successful.

It was not just other Hollywood studios that tried to capitalise on Amblin's success. Various independent production companies in the US but also in Canada, West Germany and Spain produced their own itera-tions. The films that resulted included ones in which a young boy befriends a lost alien (*Los Nuevos Extraterrestres* (*Extra-Terrestrial Visitors,* a.k.a.

*Pod People*, Juan Piquer Simon, Spain, 1983); a young boy with telekinetic powers has to fight a possessed ventriloquist doll (*Making Contact*, West Germany); extra-terrestrial gophers are hunted by alien bounty hunters in a small American town (*Critters*, Stephen Herek, 1986); a vortex opens up in a boy's back-garden releasing little gnome-demons (*The Gate*, Tibor Takács, Canada/USA, 1987); three boys find a washed up Russian sailor and hide him from their military fathers (*Russkies*, Rick Rosenthal, 1987); a young boy is terrorised by a sentient form of electricity (*The Pulse*, Paul Golding, 1988); a boy protects a super-intelligent dog from government assassins (*Watchers*, Jon Hess, 1988); and a disabled kid is visited by an alien (*Mac & Me*).

The Amblin cycle (1982–5) begins the suburban fantastic, then, and from 1983–4 to 1988 other production companies are exploiting different aspects of the Amblin cycle, creating their own suburban fantastic films along the way. The box-office disaster that was *Mac & Me* brought the spate of suburban fantastic films in independent production companies to a stop and between 1988 and 1999, a second-cycle suburban fantastic cinema begins which is largely subordinate to the 'family film' genre of the 1990s (for example, *Hocus Pocus*, *Casper*, *Jumanji*). This 90s cycle itself ended with the box-office disappointment of *Small Soldiers* and *The Iron Giant*. But during this 90s cycle, independent cinema followed Hollywood. Trimark made a number of further iterations of the suburban fantastic: *And You Thought Your Parents Were Weird* (Tony Cookson, 1991), *Evolver* (Mark Rosman, 1995) and *Star Kid* (Manny Coto, 1997). In general, the independent productions of the 1980s tended to include greater levels of violence and terror than Hollywood productions. The Trimark films of the 90s leaned towards more family friendly material but still feature swearing, a greater degree of violence, and even nudity and references to pornography, attempting to appeal to an older teenage audience that was aging out of kid's stories.

## Semantic and Syntactic Material of the Fantastic

Suburban fantastic cinema has a large repertoire of fantastic material at its disposal, drawing on the supernatural/occult elements of horror, tropes of science fiction and science fantasy. Thus we find stories involving the uncanny transformation of otherwise normal domestic objects into elements of the fantastic: televisions that suck in the protagonists (*Poltergeist, Eerie, Indiana, Pleasantville* (Gary Ross, 1998)), possessed telephones (*Making Contact, Poltergeist II*), books that pull in the protagonists to reveal animated interiors (*The Pagemaster*), board-games that become real (*Cloak and Dagger, Jumanji, Zathura: A Space Adventure* (Jon Favreau, 2005)), and ultimately, the possession of the whole suburban house by strange presences (*Poltergeist, Pulse, the 'burbs, Monster House* (Gil Kenan, 2006)). We also find films drawing on popular cultural figures of the fantastic: aliens, often with telepathic abilities (*E.T., Explorers, Flight of the Navigator*), homunculi (*Gremlins, The Gate*), giant insects (*Honey, I Shrunk the Kids*), large undiscovered species (*Harry and the Hendersons*), witches (*Hocus Pocus*), action figures that come alive (*Small Soldiers, Toy Story* (John Lasseter, 1995)), dead pets that come alive (*Frankenweenie*, Tim Burton, 2012), and robots and robotic technology (*D.A.R.Y.L., Deadly Friend* (Wes Craven, 1986), *Making Contact, Short Circuit* (John Badham, 1986), *And You Thought Your Parents Were Weird, Evolver, Star Kid, Small Soldiers, The Iron Giant*). Two of the most disruptive elements of the fantastic are science-fictional devices that permit space travel, time-travel and alternate histories (*Back to the Future, Explorers, My Science Project* (Jonathan R. Betuel, 1985), *Flight of the Navigator, Honey, I Shrunk the Kids, Jumanji*) and supernatural vortexes that allow ghosts and demons to cross into our world from another dimension (*Poltergeist, The Gate, The Monster Squad, Casper*). In addition, the syntactic structures of the fantastic contribute a number of generic forms: the haunted house (*Poltergeist, The Gate, Pulse, Casper*), the monster movie (*Gremlins, Matinee*), the alien invader (*E.T., Explorers, Flight of the Navigator, Star Kid, The Iron Giant*), time travel (*Back to the Future, Jumanji*), and vampire horror (*Fright Night* (Tom Holland, 1985), *The Lost Boys, The Monster Squad, Fright Night Part 2* (Tommy Lee Wallace, 1988)), amongst others.

As we have already seen, the fantastic element in the suburban fantastic is not simply a formulaic revival of common popular cultural tropes. They are 'pastiches', in that they recycle familiar semantic and syntactic material associated with older, established styles, and do so purposely and intentionally. Each film pastiches (appropriates, subverts, inverts and pays homage to) these popular cultural figures and tropes in different ways. For example, Mary Shelley's *Frankenstein* – about an over-reaching scientist, the technology of bringing the dead back to life and an ugly monster that is capable of kindness – and its famous Universal studios film version (*Frankenstein* (James Whale, 1931)) are common reference points for the suburban fantastic. A camp version of Karloff's Frankenstein monster appears in *Monster Squad* when a group of suburban boys ally themselves with the original monster to defeat a set of villains led by Dracula. *Frankenweenie* offers a travesty of the Frankenstein myth when a pre-teen Victor Frankenstein (Charlie Tahan) resurrects his dead dog. *Weird Science* parodies the story when two boys perform an experiment to create an ideal woman. *The Goonies* alludes to it when a deformed criminal who is ostracised by his family, responds to the kindness of the heroes. And *The Iron Giant* arguably recreates some of the force of the original story, in its depiction of an alien robot with terrible powers who becomes the victim of society's fear of his power (for more rewritings of Frankenstein, see *Deadly Friend*, *Short Circuit*, *Evolver* and *Small Soldiers*). Each deployment of this figure plays upon the audience's familiarity with its previous representations and reconceives the figure to different ends. And the combination of semantic and syntactic material deriving from the fantastic mobilises different sets of themes and values for each film.

Nevertheless, these pastiches of sf, horror and adventure genres are always combined with a 'straight' melodrama to create the suburban fantastic. This melodrama is naturalised, meaning it is never foregrounded as a genre or made subject to parody. To pastiche the melodrama would be to attack the audience's identification with the protagonist and undermine the basis of the narrative. For example, in *Back to the Future*, Marty's journey towards masculinity is played straight to facilitate audience identification. It is contrasted however, with his attempt to re-masculinise his own father, which is part of a pastiche of 50s melodrama and provokes laughter. The generic blend of 'straight' melodrama and genre pastiche is duplicated in the syntactic opposition between the internal dilemmas of the protagonist and the unknown mysteries of the outer fantastical world. The pastiches, like the element of the fantastic, are intrusions into and accelerations of what is otherwise a straight melodrama about the protagonist's upbringing. Without the element of the fantastic, suburban fantastic films would become conventional pre-teen melodramas in suburban settings. If, conversely, the element of the fantastic dominates the melodrama, the story becomes a disturbing tale of over-imagination. This happens at times in *Cloak and Dagger*, where Davey, the pre-teen protagonist, becomes involved in a real spy conspiracy, but is accompanied along the way by appearances of secret agent Jack Flack that are obviously pure fantasy. Davey's vicarious desire for 'adventure' leads him into an unnerving situation in which he shoots a man dead and ends up kidnapped on a plane with a bomb. Unintentionally, the film validates the suspicions of Davey's father about Davey's over-active imagination and implies that he is genuinely disturbed, even psychotic. This film represents an extreme; usually, the suburban fantastic finds a balance between melodrama and the fantastic: the fantastic is actually taking place in a recognisable naturalistic everyday reality but is also metaphorically implied to be a subjective fantasy.

*Forms of Melodrama*

The 'straight' melodrama of the suburban fantastic involves a hybrid drama of maturation and socialisation. Maturation narratives are apparent in the literary tradition of *bildungsroman*, and in the child characters of small-town family films of the 1940s (see Brown 2012: 85–8), while socialisation narratives are more clearly seen in heroic action adventures. A number of different narrative forms, such as fairy tale narratives, coming of age narratives, and male-focused melodramas that are resolved with the hero's triumph or victory, blend maturation and socialisation narratives together.

The process of 'natural' maturation is evident in the way that suburban fantastic films draw on typical, even universal, experiences of children. For example, suburban fantastic cinema draws on a psychological and sociological reality experienced by children; specifically, the idea that objects have a life of their own and that there exist creatures that combine the human and the animal. Jack Zipes, in his analysis of fairy tales, reminds us of Jean Piaget's characterisation of children between six and eight:

> children believe in the magical relationship between thought and things, regard inanimate objects as animate, respect authority in the form of retributive justice and expiatory punishment, see causality as paratactic, do not distinguish the self from the external world, and believe that objects can be moved in continual response to their desires. This animism and egocentrism gives way to socialization and greater conscious interaction in society

by age 10 and so the fairy tale is generally rejected by that point. They have acclimated to the real world and view the fairy tale as an impediment to further adjustment. (Zipes 2012: 175)

Suburban fantastic films often represent the time in life when children are between such animistic belief and mature adult perspectives. The residual animistic belief or magical thinking of pre-teens is apparent in scenes in which the bedroom toys of a child come alive through the presence of the element of the fantastic. *E.T.* and its imitators like *Los Nuevos Extraterrestres* and *Mac & Me*, exemplify the pleasurable side of toys coming 'alive' but other films such as *Close Encounters, Making Contact, Poltergeist II* and *Small Soldiers* are alert to the more mature perspective that experiences this as something uncanny and disturbing, even terrifying. Such scenes draw on the sociological reality of children's suburban lives in that the toys coming alive are often *real* toys that the audience would potentially own themselves. Furthermore, such real soft toys are evoked by the puppetry that creates creatures such as E.T., Gizmo, Bigfoot and the aliens in *Explorers* and *Flight of the Navigator*, and children's plastic action figures are obviously evoked by CGI equivalents such as the toys of *Toy Story* and the Gorgonites in *Small Soldiers*. Thus, some of the most popular characters in suburban fantastic cinema are subsequently marketed back to kids

The cluttered interior of a typical pre-teen male's bedroom in *Explorers* (Joe Dante, 1985).

as toys so that they can own an *E.T.* soft toy and buy an *Iron Giant* action figure, and such toys often featured electronic functions, enhancing their ability to appear 'life-like'. The appearance of fantastical creatures in suburbia, then, is not merely a trope of science fantasy. It is a residue of the fading phenomenological reality of children's lives, that inanimate objects can be secretly alive and that fantastical creatures exist. This particular separation of fantasy and reality is part of a 'natural' process of maturation that simply takes a form specific to children's lives from the 1980s onwards.

However, as children leave behind these beliefs, they enter a process that will socialise them for adult life. Therefore, suburban fantastic cinema conveys not just the 'natural' maturation of the characters, but their culturally-specific *socialisation* as well. For example, suburban fantastic films draw on 'birth of the hero' melodramas found across male-focused adventure cinema (including in sf, fantasy and horror films). Suburban fantastic cinema expresses the protagonist's journey from childhood, not just to conventional adult maturity but to a heroic masculinity that reflects an ideal socialisation of future members of society. In the 1980s, muscled über-males (such as Arnold Schwarzenegger and Sylvester Stallone) of contemporary action cinema (see Jeffords 1994) offered the ideal image of successful male socialisation. They disavowed the vulnerability and fear that was otherwise manifested by the pre-teen boys of suburban fantastic cinema. However, in the 1990s, this representational split within masculinity was symbolically healed when such figures were paired off in buddy action films such as *Terminator 2: Judgment Day* (James Cameron, 1991) and *The Last Action Hero* (John McTiernan, 1993), films which incorporated narrative elements of the suburban fantastic.

The protagonists, then, are in an awkward in-between zone, where they are still (just) engaged with outdated animism and magical thinking but are now also exposed to the genuinely adult world, whose violence and horror appears fantastic and threatening to them, but to which they must become reconciled. Of course, in any given suburban fantastic film, it is difficult to separate maturation from socialisation. For example, the normal childish fears of mysterious neighbours (*Fright Night*, *The 'burbs*, *The Monster Squad*, *Home Alone* (Chris Columbus, 1990)), criminals (*The Goonies*, *Home Alone*) and poisonous spiders (*Arachnaphobia*) are often co-opted into heightened 'fantastic' narratives, in which the protagonists learn to get over their fears of these objects. Yet this resolution often evokes more than just a 'natural' overcoming of fear. The heightened 'fantastic' nature of these normal childish fears turns the overcoming of fear into a process of socialisation into the dominant norms and values of an uncanny contemporary society.

*Suburban Iconography: Comfort, Fear, Wonder*

Suburban fantastic cinema also draws on a repertoire of semantic material involving the iconography of small towns and suburbia, familiar from small-town family films, suburban sitcoms, suburban satires, and popular culture generally. As we have seen, the small-town iconography of 1940s family films evoked feelings of stability, comfort and safety, and this was passed onto depictions of suburbia in the 1980s. Indeed, even as they pastiche suburban iconography and offer their own criticisms of suburbia through the intrusion of the fantastic, the small town and small town iconography of suburban fantastic films perpetuates this feeling of safety and comfort. But by combining pastiches of 1940s–50s suburban iconography with 1940s–50s sf and horror pastiches, suburban fantastic films deploy this iconography with a new purpose. They imply that the existence of comfortable white suburbia is grounded in the real-world analogues of the sf horrors in 1950s B-movies; that is, in the existential fear of nuclear war and other scientific and technological developments that formed the socio-historical background to the period.

The comfort and security of suburbia, then, is combined in suburban fantastic cinema with the fear, excitement, suspense and terror associated with 1950s B-movies and this creates an uncanny exchange of affects. Because these elements of the fantastic are familiar in some way (i.e. familiar from sf, horror and adventure films of the 1950s), the fantastic is also imbued with a sense of comfort that can be experienced by an audience even if they are otherwise unaware of the originals that are being pastiched. Meanwhile, the fear, terror and suspense of 1950s B-movies is absorbed into the suburban iconography, creating a pleasingly unnerving effect to the representation of everyday suburban normality. The purpose of putting together pastiches of suburban iconography and genre pastiches is to deliver this combination of comfort and fear to the audience. The audience views the films, safe in the knowledge that the horrors they show are pastiches from many previous movies and can therefore be treated ironically. However, they also have the thrill of seeing their complacency duplicated by the protagonists who are being flattered into a false sense of safety just when new terrors are bursting forth. The implication for the audience is that they are also being flattered into a false sense of safety by their cosy suburban existence and that some real socio-political terror is now bursting forth at them.

People look to the sky in raptures in *Cocoon* (Ron Howard, 1985).

This new terror is precisely the emerging socio-political dispensation of the 1980s. If small town iconography in the 1940s and 50s conveys comfort and security, and images of the fantastic convey the terror and horror of socio-political changes that continued into the 60s and 70s, then the combination of affects in the suburban fantastic films of the 1980s expresses a new structure of feeling particular to the period. As detailed by George Ritzer, the 1980s saw the expansion of cathedrals of capitalism, such as shopping malls, luxury cruise ships, theme parks and Disney movies that provoked in consumers new feelings of enchantment and wonder. A sense of materialistic transcendence, of resolved relations and identities was created in consumers by the spectacle of capitalist plenty. The suburban fantastic's unique combination of terror with wonder is an ambiguous affective mix that approximates the feeling of this new hyper-accelerated turbo-capitalism of the Reagan era, a form of capitalism that has continued to the present day.

Correspondingly, therefore, suburban fantastic cinema adds a powerful sublime affect to its older affects of comfort and fear. This is the feeling of *wonder* or *enchantment* that is so characteristic of *E.T.* and other suburban fantastic films. It is particular to this sub-genre, without a root in small-town melodrama or films of the fantastic. Instead this wonder derives from sf spectaculars like *2001: A Space Odyssey* and is brought to earth in Spielberg's *Close Encounters of the Third Kind* and domesticated in *E.T.*, from whence it is then deployed in subsequent suburban fantastic films in forms related to the magical happy endings of fairy tales or the glorious victory at the end of hero narratives. But the socio-political ground of this feeling is the celebration of what Vivian Sobchack calls 'the consumable artifacts and specular productions of late capitalism' (Sobchack 1997: 253). This is the terror that is bursting forth at the audience in suburban fantastic films, a terror that is stared at with a sense of transcendent joy.

*Experimenting with the Model*

Even as the suburban fantastic established itself as a semantic and syntactic blend, with the defining syntactic trait of a connection between the pre-teen protagonists and the element of the fantastic, it became subject to a series of experiments and extensions that altered its semantic and syntactic set. Most obviously, suburban iconography was increasingly avoided in favour of small towns, in-land and coastal, with older architectural styles. *Starman* and *Flight of the Navigator* swap single towns for road trip narratives. *SpaceCamp* takes place entirely at Cape Canaveral and in orbit, but the characters' personal dilemmas and the film's connection to the element of the fantastic (being launched into space) align it with the suburban fantastic. *batteries not included* and the sequels to *Poltergeist*, *Gremlins* and *Fright Night* all relocate to cities, swapping the suburban for the urban.

The fantastic too was also subject to alteration. The desire to keep the suburban fantastic alive as a semantic/syntactic model encouraged studios to switch from the fantastic genres of sf, horror and fantasy to pastiches of other generic forms, such as adventure (*The Goonies*, *The Pagemaster*, *Jumanji*), military drama (*Red Dawn*, *Russkies*, *Matinee*, *Small Soldiers*, *The Iron Giant*), Disney-style family film (*Flight of the Navigator*) and *Rear Window*-type detective mysteries (*The 'burbs*, *Monster House*). Some of these combinations arguably depart from the realm of the fantastic. *The Karate Kid* could be seen as suburban fantastic, except that the element of the fantastic has been replaced by a pastiche of martial arts/sports genres. *The Last Starfighter*, in which a teenager is kidnapped by an alien race to pilot a ship in an intergalactic war, combines teenage melodrama with *Star Wars*-style space opera, but leans towards the space opera more than the suburban fantastic. Despite these changes, *The Karate Kid* and *The Last Starfighter* arguably maintain the connection between the protagonist's dilemmas and the intrusion of a form of fantastic (oriental sports/space adventure) that defines the suburban fantastic. But *Red Dawn* separates the protagonists' imaginations from the element of the fantastic (the invasion of Soviet army) and so is ultimately more of a war melodrama featuring teenage characters than a suburban fantastic film.

Other films similarly abandon the underlying male melodrama in the suburban fantastic and offer melodramas influenced by other suburban-set sub-genres of the 1980s and 90s, such as the pet movie, the vacation movie, the Christmas movie, the summer camp movie, and the city-adventure movie. For example, *Adventures in Babysitting* (Chris Columbus, 1987) side-lines the television-watching pre-teen boys of its narrative to focus on a teenage girl's journey into the city that is literal and not imaginary. And *Big* (Penny Marshall, 1988) follows a suburban teenage boy who magically turns into an adult and heads to the city to become an employee in a corporate toy company. These variations establish suburban fantastic cinema as a sub-cycle within the larger category of 'family film', that became prominent in the 1990s.

All of these different types of alteration combine to create strong tonal variation across this set of films. The representation of suburban culture shifts from being sympathetic (*The Sandlot, Jumanji*), to subtly critical (*E.T.*), to openly satirical (*Poltergeist, Gremlins, The 'burbs*). The depiction of character-based melodrama shifts from being serious and sentimental (*E.T., Flight of the Navigator, Honey I Shrunk the Kids, Jumanji, The Iron Giant*) to being pastiches of 50's teen melodrama (*Back to the Future, Edward Scissorhands* (Tim Burton, 1990), *Matinee, Pleasantville*). In fact, the tone of suburban fantastic films ranges across tragedy (*Red Dawn*), zany comedy (*Weird Science*), fairy tale (*Edward Scissorhands*), Spielbergian wonder and pathos (*E.T., Cocoon, Flight of the Navigator, Harry and the Hendersons*), camp (*The Monster Squad, Hocus Pocus*), and sentimental nostalgia (*The Sandlot, Matinee, The Iron Giant*).

Although many of these films move beyond the suburban setting, the genres of sf, horror and fantasy, the male melodrama, and the tonal mix of the Amblin cycle, they generally retain the distinctive connection between the pre-teen protagonist's personal dilemmas and the element of the fantastic. Therefore, in my view, films in which this remains the domi-nant element in their generic mix may be called 'suburban fantastic films', although careful analysis is required to determine each film's relationship to this semantic/syntactic model.

In any case, the generic uncertainty of some of these films is not a consequence of the suburban fantastic model, but of the Hollywood genre system itself, whereby generic signals are deployed as part of a film's marketing in order to attract the widest possible audience (see Altman 1999: 44–8). Many films released in the period after *E.T.* and other Amblin hits were marketed and framed as if they would also deliver something of the tone and feel of an Amblin film or a suburban fantastic film, even though their narrative content was often radically different. For example, *Ghostbusters* does not support our definition of the suburban fantastic, yet it involves the supernatural, it was marketed to kids and was scary enough for pre-teens to watch without being too scary. Many films of the 80s and 90s were similarly framed. Children's fantasy films like *Return to Oz* (Walter Murch, 1985), *Labyrinth* (Jim Henson, 1986) and *The Princess Bride* (Rob Reiner, 1987) were marketed to the same audience demographic as *E.T.*

and included characters and tropes common to suburban fantastic films, but they can also be interpreted as children's fantasies, similar to pre-*E.T.* films such as *Mary Poppins* and *Willy Wonka*. Such films are associated with the suburban fantastic on the basis of the proximity of their release to suburban fantastic films, their shared audience demographic (mainly pre-teen and teenager), and a certain continuity of style in their marketing (posters, VHS packaging, trailers), even though it is clear that these films have quite different semantic and syntactic content. Rick Altman reminds us that the genre of a film alters over the course of its reception and the existence of films that are marketed to capitalise on the success of Amblin's films helps us distinguish the semantic and syntactic blend that constitutes the suburban fantastic more clearly (Altman 1999: 77–82).

With that in mind, it is worth noting a set of films which are set in suburbia and feature elements of the fantastic but which do *not* qualify as suburban fantastic according to our definition. In films like *My Stepmother is an Alien* (Richard Benjamin, 1988), *Parents* (Bob Balaban, 1989), *Meet the Applegates* (Michael Lehmann, 1991), *The Coneheads* (Steve Barron, 1993) and *Serial Mom* (John Waters, 1994), the connection between the consciousness of the protagonists and the element of the fantastic is absent. Indeed, pre-teens are generally side-lined as protagonists in favour of adults and these films entirely lack the distinctive tonal blend of horror and sentiment pioneered by Amblin. Instead, these films are satires of suburban living that use exaggerated or hyperbolic situations (cannibalism, alien colonisation, serial killing) for comical effect. The element of the fantastic is the expression of the secretly deviant nature of suburban culture, rather than the projection of a protagonist's personal melodramas. These suburban satires films have more in common with other satires of contemporary life than they do with the suburban fantastic. The suburban setting and the genre of the fantastic is not enough to establish the distinctive connection between the protagonist and the element of the fantastic in the suburban fantastic.

*Case Study: Making Contact (a.k.a. Joey) (1985)*

Close attention to Roland Emmerich's West German film *Making Contact* can indicate just how established the semantic and syntactic blend of the suburban fantastic had become, even by 1985. Emmerich's film was released as *Joey* in Germany in a 98 minute version, but in the US it appeared as *Making Contact* in a 79 minute edit. The longer, German version constitutes the fullest imitation up to that point of the semantic and syntactic mix evident in Amblin's box-office successes and showcases the skill with popular genres that led Emmerich to a successful career directing Hollywood sf blockbusters. Although it was not a hit in the States and is largely forgotten now, *Making Contact* reveals how desperately some filmmakers wanted to copy the semantic and syntactic mix of the Amblin films.

Filmed in Germany, *Making Contact* is nevertheless set in an 'American' town and tells of a young boy, Joey (Joshua Morrell), whose father has recently died. He wishes that his dad would return and this wish prompts the spirit of his father to communicate with him through a toy telephone. It also makes all the toys in his bedroom come to life, including a robot called Charlie who seems to become permanently alive. Although this might be enough for Joey to overcome his grief, the film then introduces a malevolent force. In a spooky boarded-up house neighbouring his home, Joey finds a ventriloquist doll possessed by the spirit of Fletcher, a vaudeville performer of the 1930s and 40s who died mysteriously in 1954 after killing his wife and child. The doll wants to 'play a game' with him and when Joey refuses the doll terrorises him by possessing objects, shooting electricity, controlling all the lights in the house, and taking control of a car. He even turns Joey's bedroom closet into a smoky vortex with light in a genuinely unnerving scene, which is all the more unnerving since the doll's powers are not clearly distinguished from the father's benevolent spiritual presence.

Joey, then, is caught in a struggle for his soul between two spirits, that of his dead father and that of the possessed doll with telekinetic powers. Joey realises that to end the doll's reign of terror, he has to play the doll's game. He enters the spooky house next door which internally collapses to reveal a magical maze in which Joey and his friends are challenged by a big lizard monster, a mummy, a hamburger with teeth, Darth Vader, and a giant version of Fletcher (it's implied that the doll is making their worst fears come true). At the centre of the maze, Joey is confronted with the spirit of his father and the doll. The father indicates an exit from the maze but when Joey opens it, he discovers a shining light, mountains and mist – a vision of heaven, where Joey could join his dead father. Joey chooses his father and at that moment, light shoots through the doorway and destroys the doll. Joey then goes through the door to heaven and when he is found in the spooky house and given CPR, he appears to have already died. However, the final scene of the film, in which all the toys in his room start coming to life again, make it clear that Joey has returned to life, renewed by his father's spirit.

Making Contact, then, clearly duplicates key elements of the suburban fantastic. Joey's grief over his father's death is correlated with the appearance of the fantastic in his life. By drawing on the strength of his father's spirit, he defeats the doll in the symbolic maze of grief, overcomes his own longing to die, and returns to life. Where suburban fantastic films emphasise social melodramas of growing up, Emmerich stresses the starker existential issues of life versus death, which perhaps accounts for some of the intensity of the film. Scenes which could either provoke wonder and fear in the audience often provoke both at the same time.

Within this frame, Emmerich also puts into play many suburban fantastic tropes that were already well established enough by 1985 to be imitated. He shows a child combating a supernatural possessed doll, as in *Poltergeist*, while also showing him engaging with a benevolent spirit that gives him telekinetic powers, akin to *E.T.* The invasion of the house by the government scientists and the false death of Joey and his resurrection at the end are recognisable from *E.T.* Charlie, the toy robot who becomes 'possessed' by life, evokes the many toy robots and cute creatures that appear from *Gremlins* onwards. The sub-plot involving a group of neighbouring boys playing military games and spying on the government recalls the protagonists of *The Goonies*. Indeed, at times, it seems as if Emmerich is intent on duplicating as many Amblin tropes as he can, without worrying about how well they work together in a single plot.

Emmerich also imitates the stylistic aspects of Spielberg's film-making. There are frequent hill-rise shots of kids on bicycles against the sun, of nightscapes over suburbia, of smoke-machines and construction lights, and Spielbergian faces of wonder. And Joey also has an American-style boys bedroom, with *Sesame Street* curtains, American sports paraphernalia, *E.T.* wallpaper in his cupboard, and a *Return of the Jedi* (Richard Marquand, 1983) duvet. *Making Contact* shows how quickly *Star Wars* and *E.T.* became meta-references that could be deployed within a suburban fantastic film in place of references to the 1950s science fiction cinema. Its blend of the tones of *Poltergeist* and *E.T.* unbalance its storytelling but *Making Contact* has a raw power and visual appeal that anticipates Emmerich's future success in Hollywood.

*The Suburban Fantastic as a Subordinate Element in a Generic Mix*

Once the suburban fantastic was established as an ongoing semantic and syntactic blend, it joined a pool of generic possibilities and came to be deployed as a subordinate element within films that alternatively backgrounded pre-teen protagonists, the suburban setting, and the relationship between the consciousness of the protagonist and the fantastic, in favour of semantic and syntactic material from pre-established genres. The suburban fantastic had become so widespread by this point that important aspects of suburban fantastic narratives often appeared as subordinate elements in films in which other genres were dominant. It would be difficult to account for all the established genres with which the semantic and syntactic material of suburban fantastic cinema has been co-joined, but we can identify a number of general trends.

*As Teen Movies*

For example, the development of suburban fantastic cinema occurs in parallel with the growth of teen movies from the late 1970s. The proximity in age between the pre-teen characters of suburban fantastic cinema and the teenage characters of teen movies, as well as their shared location within suburbia, meant that teen-focused films were natural venues in which further permutations of the suburban fantastic model could be developed. Furthermore, teenagers are at a stage in life where they are escaping from their immediate suburban surroundings to high school, to the shopping mall and urban life. This permits teen movies to blend semantic and syntactic material from the suburban fantastic model with established genres like romance, high school story, comedy, melodrama and horror, such that the suburban fantastic material becomes subordinate to more established genres. Teen-focused films such as *Wargames* (John Badham, 1983), *Gremlins*, *Red Dawn*, *A Nightmare on Elm Street*, *Night of the Comet* (Thom Eberhardt, 1984), *The Last Starfighter*, *My Science Project*, *Back to the Future*, *Teen Wolf* (Rod Daniel, 1985), *Once Bitten* (Howard Storm, 1985), *The Wraith* (Mike Marvin, 1986), *The Manhattan Project* (Marshall Brickman, 1986), *Deadly Friend* and *Beetlejuice* (Tim Burton, 1988) either have clear suburban fantastic narratives or use suburban fantastic material in a subordinate fashion. Teen-focused suburban fantastic films maintain the distinctive connection between the personal melodramas of the protagonists and the element of the fantastic disrupting suburbia, but change the semantic material greatly. In teen-focused films with only some elements of the suburban fantastic, the main protagonist is as likely to be female as male, and the elements of the fantastic are invested with adult psycho-sexual anxieties to a greater degree than they are in pre-teen suburban fantastic films. Typically, male-focused sex/body melodramas are played for laughs (*Teen Wolf, Fright Night, Once Bitten*), but when female-focused, they are taken seriously (*A Nightmare on Elm Street*).

In this regard, we should mention *Halloween* (John Carpenter, 1978) as a notable precursor to the suburban fantastic. The box-office success of John Carpenter's teenage-focused suburban horror film established the suburban horror or 'slasher' film, in which the personal and sexual melodramas of an often female teenager are accompanied by the intrusive presence of a supernatural serial killer, who terrorises the heroine and kills many of her friends. The heroine's personal dilemmas are only resolved by their final confrontation with the killer. The influence of Carpenter's film has been in the direction of teen-focused slasher horror films, some of the best of which are set in suburbia and include aspects of the suburban fantastic in their generic complex (see *A Nightmare on Elm Street* and its sequels, *Scream* (Wes Craven, 1996) and its sequels).

## As an Adult-focused Suburban Fantastic

Nor were teenagers the only other demographic that could be addressed through the suburban fantastic. Murray Pomerance notes that modern society blurs the distinction between childhood and adulthood (Pomerance 2004: 133–4), so teenagers, young adults and even adults can all be suitable protagonists for child-focused films. After John Carpenter's *Starman*, it was clear that adult protagonists and concerns were not limited to suburban gothic style melodramas but could constitute the focus of suburban fantastic narratives. In general, however, suburban fantastic cinema has eschewed realistic representations of adult concerns and represented adults through a child's idea of what adults are like. They are, in Brown and Babington's term, 'symbolic children', 'mutable, ambivalent figures, embodying values of innocence, play and superficial anarchism' (Brown and Babington 2015: 4).

Consequently, zany, comic fathers become crucial protagonists in *Harry and the Hendersons*, *The 'burbs*, *Honey, I Shrunk the Kids* and *Jumanji*. Mothers and women in general tend to be side-lined in the suburban fantastic (*Flight of the Navigator*, *The 'burbs*, *Home Alone*, *The Iron Giant*). *Invaders from Mars* (Tobe Hooper, 1986) and *Watchers* are rare instances of pairing a male pre-teen protagonist with a maternal sidekick. And child-like grandparents became the focus in *Cocoon* and *\*batteries not included*.

The consequence of focusing on adult characters and their connection to the fantastic is that pre-teens are often displaced to the side-lines with only residual connections to the fantastic. The pre-teens Ernie (Joshua Rudoy) in *Harry and the Hendersons*, Dave (Cory Danziger) in *The 'burbs*, and David (Barret Oliver) in *Cocoon* display such residual connections. For example, in *Cocoon*, the elderly residents of a care home discover an alien re-aging power that allows them to regain their youth and overcome illness. The story is focused on three old men and a young adult (Steve Guttenberg) who helps the aliens retrieve their life-giving eggs from the sea. However, the film begins with David, the pre-teen grandson of Ben (Wilford Brimley) and Mary (Maureen Stapleton), looking at the stars through a telescope. This implies a connection between David's imagination and the aliens that subsequently appear. David's issue is that he doesn't have any friends, so he hangs out with his grandpa. But when Ben and Mary leave with the aliens at the end, David accepts their departure and symbolically loses his fear of other people. The film ends with David at their funeral confident that they have transcended to a higher plane. David's presence, then, supplements the story of the elderly regaining their youth, with a story about a grandson overcoming the loss of his grandparents. A young boy's maturation/socialisation is accelerated by the fantastic, but it is no longer the centre of the story.

*As a Subordinate Mode in the Modern Blockbuster*

Suburban fantastic cinema also has a symbiotic relationship with adult-centric blockbuster spectacle. The emergence of the modern blockbuster (contemporary monster movies, alien invasion movies, space operas) in the late 1970s and 1980s relegated an older set of sf, horror, fantasy and action-adventure films of the 1950s and this allowed them to become objects of pastiche in the suburban fantastic. Reciprocally, the suburban

A T-Rex explores suburbia in *The Lost World: Jurassic Park* (Steven Spielberg, 1997).

fantastic itself was drawn into the new contemporary sf, horror, fantasy and action-adventure films as a subordinate element. Although in these films, suburban fantastic material is overwhelmed by other generic material, Rick Altman reminds us that a single semantic or syntactic element – the presence of a pre-teen protagonist, an sf, horror or fantasy element, an implicit connection between the two, or even merely a blend of comfort, fear and wonder – may be enough to resurrect in the audience's mind the feel of the genre (Altman 1999: 132). For example, a short vignette late in *The Lost World: Jurassic Park* (Steven Spielberg, 1997) offers all the key elements of the suburban fantastic. A boy wakes up in his suburban home to see out the window a Tyrannosaurus Rex drinking out of the back pool. When he tries to wake his parents, they dismiss his warning as a fantasy until the T-Rex appears staring in their bedroom window and they scream. The combination of the boy's point of view, the appearance of a living T-Rex in suburbia, the parents' disbelief, and the confirmation of the boy's assertion is a concentrated example of the major semantic and syntactic elements of the suburban fantastic deployed within a monster adventure movie.

The simplest way to introduce some of the semantic and syntactic material of the suburban fantastic into modern blockbusters, however, is to introduce pre-teen protagonists who form important sidekicks to the main heroes. This leads to films in which a young boy is hunted by robots from the future who think he is the future saviour of mankind (*Terminator 2: Judgment Day*); in which a discontented boy obsessed with cinema is transported into the latest action film with his screen hero (*The Last Action Hero*); and in which a brother and sister visit a dinosaur park which breaks down and releases the dinosaurs (*Jurassic Park*). As with adult-focused suburban fantastic films, the fantasies of these pre-teens remain secondary to the adult protagonist's encounter with the fantastic. Instead, the children function partly as stand-ins for that audience demographic, since, despite adult ratings, blockbusters are often marketed to children as well and have accompanying toy lines. But these films still imply a connection between children's imaginations and fantastic events, even as they are careful to confirm the objective reality of the fantastic.

*Aligning Audience and Product*

Although the number of suburban fantastic films are sufficient in my view to constitute a significant sub-genre, it is obvious that over almost forty years the number of films in which the suburban fantastic is the dominant generic trait remains quite small. It has never become as common as the disaster film or action film or western. Yet the small set of suburban fantastic films and its tendency to continually reappear tells us something about its status within Hollywood's generic economy of the last forty years. The fact is that suburban fantastic cinema isn't merely one more sub-genre amongst all the others. Unlike other sub-genres, suburban fantastic cinema is the place where Hollywood represents to itself the ultimate destination of its own products (suburbia) and its key audience demographic (suburban-dwelling male pre-teens and teens). The real-life circumstance by which a Hollywood movie intrudes into the normal suburban life of pre-teens and colonises their imaginations with the tropes of sf, fantasy, horror, adventure and other pre-established genres, is duplicated in the protagonists' encounter with an element of the fantastic, which is both objectively real in their world, but also implicitly a product of their own imagination. Suburban fantastic films, then, dramatise the relationship between the film-going audience and Hollywood's generic products. This is indicated by the correspondence between the choice of fantastic at any given moment and the pre-dominance of certain blockbusters at the box-office. Where *Poltergeist* responds to the new intense horror films of the

1970s such as *The Exorcist* and *The Omen*, *Home Alone* likewise responds to the success of 'under siege' action films like *Die Hard* (John McTiernan, 1988). *Jumanji* is clearly responding to the success of *Jurassic Park* by melding the suburban setting with a jungle-based CGI-animal extravaganza, while *Zathura: A Space Adventure* is reacting to the success of disaster movies like *Armageddon* (1998). The pre-existing genres utilised within the suburban fantastic are in dialogue with the developmental progression of Hollywood's most successful genres of the day (as well as with the changing sociological terrain of the suburban market); therefore, we can read into the changing genre pastiches Hollywood's changing way of understanding the audience and destination of its products. When suburban fantastic films show the protagonists solving their personal melodramas through their struggle with the element of the fantastic, we can also see Hollywood fantasising about the positive effect of its products on the audience and the world. It imagines that the intoxicating power of its films resolves the protagonist's identity in an ultimate fulfilment of desire. The real effect of Hollywood images on the audience, however, may be quite different and the potential negative effect of cinematic images and media images in general are represented in the more satirical suburban fantastic films (*Poltergeist*, *Gremlins*, *The 'burbs*, *Matinee*, etc.). These come closer to acknowledging that the protagonist's reception of these images is not part of an idealised maturation, but a process of socialisation that resolves them as consumers, who will be ready to consume further Hollywood genres and all the other enchanting commodities that are condensed in particular instances of the fantastic.

It is for this reason, then, that the canon of suburban fantastic films produced over the 1980s and 1990s remains relatively small. Hollywood produces suburban fantastic films periodically in response to fluctuations in the popularity of its blockbuster genres, and the popularity of suburban fantastic films reassures Hollywood that the world of its consumers remains aligned with its products. No other sub-genre allows Hollywood to visualise its key audience demographic's relationship to Hollywood products to the same extent.

*Conclusion*

Variations of the suburban fantastic model were a necessary development for its perpetuation, since after the box-office failure of *Mac & Me*, it was clear that adhering closely to the *E.T.* model was no longer enough for audiences. Luckily, by this point, the suburban fantastic had become established as a semantic and syntactic set of great flexibility, one which could be present in the background of a film's generic mix or could predominate to such a level that it constituted a distinctive sub-genre. Films in which the semantic and syntactic elements of the suburban fantastic were dominant were some of the highest grossing films of the period. *Honey, I Shrunk the Kids* was a huge sleeper hit for Disney in 1989, the fifth highest grossing film of that year. And 1990 saw *Home Alone*, scripted by John Hughes who had written *Weird Science*, and directed by Chris Columbus, who wrote *Gremlins* and *The Goonies*, become the number one highest grossing hit of the year. Together they established a second cycle of the suburban fantastic which throughout the 1990s inspired various family films (*Hocus Pocus*, *The Pagemaster*, *Casper*, *Jumanji*, *Small Soldiers*, *The Iron Giant*), in which the semantic and syntactic material of the suburban fantastic dominated. Even suburban fantastic films with moderate or low box office returns (*Hocus Pocus*, *The Iron Giant*, *Zathura: A Space Adventure*) and lower budget independent productions (*The Gate*, *Pulse*) went on, like their more-successful cousins, to have long lives on VHS, watched and rewatched countless times by a whole generation of children. Indeed, the development of the new lucrative home video market through the 1980s and the existence of a captive domestic audience of children, ensured that suburban fantastic movies were amongst the best-selling titles. The intensity with which these films were rewatched is not a neutral phenomenon, however. Rather it caused these films to become an important part of the socialisation process experienced by children growing up in the late twentieth century.

## 3    MASCULINITY

The various elements of the fantastic that intrude into suburban spaces are intimately related to the specific personal, familial and fraternal melodramas of the main pre-teen protagonist. The protagonist feels a sense of inadequacy and is acting-out because of some fundamental discontent. They are troubled by fear and anxiety over social dramas of friendship, family, school, bullying and love: the sense of dislocation from moving house (*The Lost Boys, Hocus Pocus, Jumanji*); the process of coming to terms with parental divorce or separation (*E.T., Zathura*); the death of a parent (*Cloak and Dagger, Jumanji*); the arrival of a new neighbour (*Fright Night*); alienation from the family (*Flight of the Navigator, Jumanji, Small Soldiers*); the challenge of making and keeping new friends (*The Lost Boys, Hocus Pocus, The Hole*); the threat of bullies (*Explorers, Back to the Future, Hocus Pocus, Jumanji*); and the strange new feelings of attraction and desire (*The Goonies, Fright Night, Weird Science, Hocus Pocus*). Lying behind these premises is the general discontent with the limitations of being a child, a sense of maladjustment to the world. The protagonists' subsequent encounter with the fantastic dramatises the process by which these personal dilemmas are resolved happily. The protagonist's anxieties about the prospect of growing up are superseded by their acceptance of mature values such as loyalty, duty, honour, friendship, love and courage. This is framed as a process of emotional maturation, rather than one of physical maturation through puberty. And the fairy-tale quality of these resolutions makes these stories very satisfying and 'magical' to audiences.

However, this encounter with the fantastic can also be interpreted as dramatising a process of socialisation, in which the protagonist is encountering specifically patriarchal values and discourses and is experiencing an existential identity crisis at the knowledge of this patriarchal inheritance. This crisis ends when the protagonist comes to a new compromise with this patriarchal inheritance, in parallel with expelling the fantastic from suburbia. Usually their new 'heroic' identity consolidates around a 'soft' version of patriarchal values (heterosexuality, male domination, and conservative notions of gender identity). He establishes his heroic masculinity by saving himself and people close to him. But some suburban fantastic films take this further. The new 'heroic' identity is consolidated around harder forms of patriarchy (power, violence, exploitation). Although the protagonists are discontented by the parental order, their encounter with the fantastic leads them to accept and internalise a new 'violent' heroism, with the implication that they will propagate it in their adult lives. Suburban fantastic films, then, generally couple a romanticisation of boyhood with 'the details of socialization, the mechanism of the transfer of power, the roots of the presumption of gender superiority, the foundations of "boys' nature"' (Pomerance and Gateward 2004: 2).

### The Male Hegemony of the Suburban Fantastic

It cannot be ignored that, unlike children's fantasy stories generally, the suburban fantastic privileges males, specifically white, middle-class and implicitly or explicitly heterosexual males, for its heroes. As examples, we may recall Eliot in *E.T.*, Mikey (Sean Austin), Mouth (Corey Feldman) and Chunk (Jeff Cohen) in *The Goonies*, Ben (Ethan Hawke) and Wolfgang (River Phoenix) in *Explorers*, Gary (Anthony Michael Hall) and Wyatt (Ilan Mitchell-Smith) in *Weird Science*, David (Joey Cramer) in *Flight of the Navigator*, Sean (Andre Gower) and Patrick (Robby Kiger) in *The Monster Squad*, Sam (Corey Haim) and the Frog Brothers (Jamison Newlander, Corey Feldman) in *The Lost Boys*, Gene (Simon Fenton) and Stan (Omri Katz) in *Matinee*, Alan (Adam Hann-Byrd) in *Jumanji*, and Alan (Gregory Smith) in *Small Soldiers*. This male focus is not a neutral bias. In fact, it fundamentally shapes the types of character melodrama in suburban fantastic films.

*Father-Son and Family Melodrama*

For example, father-son relationships are one of the most common forms of melodrama in suburban fantastic cinema. Often, the protagonists are being brought up by mothers with fathers absent, separated or divorced (*E.T.*, but also *Deadly Friend*, *The Lost Boys*, *The Manhattan Project*, *Watchers*, *Mac & Me*). The protagonist's psychic trauma is expressed in the form of the intrusive fantastic element, and their conflict with it allows them to resolve their feelings about this parental relationship. For example, in *E.T.*, when Elliott finally meets the lead government scientist (Peter Coyote), the scientist claims to have a similar bond to E.T. as Elliott. The scientist's transformation from apparent villainy to sympathetic help culminates in the final scene where he is placed next to Elliott's mother. The villain of the film who has been persecuting E.T. is ultimately revealed to be an older version of Elliott, and a possible surrogate father-figure. When Elliott accepts E.T.'s departure, he resolves his conflicted feelings over the absence of his father. E.T.'s symbolic father figure may be a conservative government functionary, but suburban fantastic films are just as capable of directing the protagonist towards countercultural figures as towards authority figures: in *The Iron Giant*, for example, a beatnik artist who helps pre-teen Hogarth (Eli Marienthal) hide the Giant (Vin Diesel) becomes his surrogate dad at the end.

Alternatively, the protagonist can be in conflict with the father (*Cloak and Dagger*, *Pulse*) and the melodrama then hinges on their reconciliation. For example, in *Jumanji*, Alan suffers from a conflict with his father over whether he's going to be sent to his father's former boarding school. He also has subsidiary problems – bullies, an accident in his dad's factory that he is told off for, and his bike being stolen. His anger over these issues is continually accompanied by a mysterious drum beat that comes from the Jumanji board-game. Just when he's ready to run away, he delays by playing Jumanji with Sally (Laura Bell Bundy) and ends up being sucked into the game. Alan's melodrama of 1969 is then supplemented by another in the present of 1994 involving a sister and brother, Judy (Kirsten Dunst) and Peter (Bradley Pierce), who have lost their parents and are coping with it differently. Peter has become mute to all but his sister, and she is a pathological liar. They move into Alan's old house, hear the drumbeats, find the Jumanji board-game in the attic and end up playing it as well.

Alan (Robin Williams), Judy (Kirsten Dunst) and Peter (Bradley Pierce) play the game in
*Jumanji* (1995).

This releases a now grown-up Alan (Robin Williams) from the board-game.
He discovers that because he refused the responsibility of continuing his
father's business and disappeared into the game, his father put all his
money into finding his son at the cost of the factory, which ultimately shut,
bringing destitution to the whole town's prosperity. Thus, Alan is shown
the unintended and extreme consequence of his act of resisting his father.
The moral of the story seems to be that your parents really do love you so
don't run away from responsibility, otherwise all of society will collapse.
*Jumanji* reveals the extent to which suburban fantastic films see the prosperity of the local community as wrapped up in the duty and responsibility
of the young white male as the only person who can keep society going – a
trope that goes back to *It's A Wonderful Life* (see Rowley 2015: 48).

Unfortunately, the jungle environment of Jumanji begins to penetrate
the house and Alan, Judy, Peter and grown-up Sally (Bonnie Hunt) have
to keep on playing the game to save themselves, in the process confronting their own personal problems. Part of the game involves Alan being
chased by Van Pelt (Jonathan Hyde), a hunter played by the same actor as
his father. At the climax, he stands his ground against Van Pelt and says,
'My father always said you have to face what you fear.' Van Pelt replies 'So
you've finally become a man!' At that moment, Alan wins the game and all

the animals are pulled back into the board-game. The film then jumps back to 1969. Alan and Sally are kids again and have finished the game. Now realising the consequences of his actions, Alan abandons his idea to run away and reconciles with his father. They make a new compromise. Alan won't have to go to boarding school, and he confesses that he caused the accident at the factory for which Carl (David Alan Grier) was blamed. With this confession, he secures Carl's new trainer design for the factory. Alan and Sally drown the board-game in a river and Alan receives a kiss from Sally, cementing his heterosexuality and masculinity.

Then in the coda, we jump forward to an alternative, improved present. Alan and Sarah have got married. They've kept the company going and the town is prospering. Judy and Peter visit them with their parents, but they have no memory of their adventure together. Alan and Sarah offer the parents a job in the shoe factory, thereby saving them from their accident and changing the course of Judy and Peter's lives. Thus, by Alan's new compromise with his father, renouncing the emotional coldness of boarding school but still inheriting the business, he manages to improve his own life, Sally's, his business, *and* the whole town, as well as save Judy and Peter's parents, and alter their lives for the better as well. The fairy-tale restoration of white male middle-class heterosexuality to its rightful place in society is complete. And by having the same actor playing Alan's father and the antagonist Van Pelt, and synchronising the moment the game is won with Alan claiming his masculinity, *Jumanji* makes clear that this is a specifically male melodrama about the inheritance of an acceptable gender male role.

Numerous other suburban fantastic films involve father-son conflicts. Even when fathers are absent, suburban fantastic cinema puts father-son relationships at the heart of the nuclear family and proscribes larger family units of uncles, aunts, cousins and grandparents that might dilute the focus on the father-son relationship. Extended families played a significant part in small-town family films of the 1940s, but in the suburban fantastic, the banished members of the extended family return in the figure of the spooky old neighbour (*Fright Night, Deadly Friend, The Monster Squad, Pulse, The 'burbs, Home Alone, The Sandlot, Monster House, The Hole*), a symbolic 'grandparent figure' that the nuclear family cannot accommodate but who is often belatedly revealed as a benevolent ally. These characters indicate the ideological insistence on the nuclear family, even at the expense of banishing these individuals who could otherwise form part of the family.

This father-focused nuclear family, then, is itself a synecdoche of the suburban or small-town community which forms the ideal utopian collectivity of suburban fantastic cinema. But films like *Jumanji* reveal that this collectivity is fragile and ultimately dependent on the decisions of the inheriting son. By accepting traditional masculine values (duty, hard work, responsibility), the protagonist restores their status in the family and also ensures the future prosperity of their family, the wider local society, and by implication, America itself.

*Peer Group Melodrama: Gender and Class*

Part of the male protagonist's melodrama also involves encounters with peers of different genders, classes and abilities. Alliances and friendships are made and validated during the encounter with the fantastic, but when the protagonist defeats the element of the fantastic and resolves their personal difficulties, these alliances and friendships are consolidated in different ways. Many films show the happy establishment of fraternal and romantic bonds, but some also stress that the main character's new heroic identity position him above and beyond his peers.

For example, the roles granted to female characters are invariably dependent on their relationship to the main male protagonist. Female siblings and friends between three and eight – Carol-Anne in *Poltergeist*, Gerty (Drew Barrymore) in *E.T.*, Kim (Christina Nigra) in *Cloak and Dagger*, Sally (Tamara Shields) in *Making Contact*, Phoebe (Ashley Bank) in *The Monster Squad*, Debbie (Lauren Stanley) in *Mac & Me* and Dani (Thora Birch) in *Hocus Pocus* – are granted a certain prominence in the narrative, presumably because they are sexually neutral for the protagonist. Female protagonists of the same age are firmly positioned in supporting roles as girlfriends, love interests or girl-next-door types whose love comes as a reward for the protagonist's heroism. Indeed, one of the most important functions of the female sidekick is that they resolve the protagonist's heterosexuality and masculinity with symbolic kisses. Allison (Vinessa Shaw) in *Hocus Pocus*, Sherry (Kellie Martin) and Sandra (Lisa Jakub) in *Matinee*, Sarah in *Jumanji*, Kat in *Casper*, and Christy (Kirsten Dunst) in *Small Soldiers* all perform this function for the male protagonist – and these characters feature in suburban fantastic films of the 1990s, which generally give greater attention to female characters. In *Casper*, Kat (Christina Ricci) is the main character, and in *Hocus Pocus* the focus is split between three witches who are the comic antagonists and two girls and a boy who is mocked throughout the story. However, even with this greater attention, female characters are subordinated to the agency of the male protagonists. Max (Omri Katz) releases the witches in *Hocus Pocus*, and in *Casper*, Kat's personal dilemmas are secondary to those of Casper the ghost.

Older female siblings are caricatured as the stroppy older sister – Lisa (Kristen Stewart) in *Zathura: A Space Adventure* – and older female friends are sources of attraction and erotic aspiration. In *The Goonies*, Mikey accidently receives a kiss from his brother's girlfriend Andy (Kerri Green) and in *Weird Science*, the emasculated geeks Gary and Wyatt manage to obtain older girlfriends Hilly (Judie Aronson) and Deb (Suzanne Synder) by stealing them from two bullies. With teenage male protagonists, female characters equivalent in age to the protagonist are more prominent – Kate (Phoebe Cates) in *Gremlins*, Lorraine (Lea Thompson) in *Back to the Future*, Jennifer (Ally Sheedy) in *WarGames* – but explorations of teenage sexuality are generally avoided. Such explorations are saved for teen films in which the suburban fantastic is merely one part of a generic mix.

This general subordination of female characters is surprising since melodramas of maturation (fairy tales and the coming-of-age drama) are gender non-specific. Suburban fantastic cinema's prioritisation of the maturation of male characters over female characters can only be explained as a consequence of its focus on establishing a new compromise between emerging male identities and patriarchy.

Accompanying the subordination of women and the displacement of extended family members, is the banishment of members of the lower class from the patriarchal community. Members of the lower class are figured as bullies, whose class difference is conveyed through physical type (muscular labouring stock), language, education and attitude to violence. Suburban fantastic cinema tends to naturalise this divide. The bullies are persecuting the 'innocent' protagonist and at the end, the protagonist is able to take revenge on the bully. Interestingly, the guilt of revenge is sometimes lifted off the shoulders of the protagonist and carried by the story, as when, in *Back to the Future*, Biff gets his comeuppance by driving into a truck carrying manure, an event that occurs without the persecuted hero Marty actively intending it. Suburban fantastic cinema treats such revenge as fully justified in the name of the protagonist overcoming their own timidity and weakness, a process capped at the end through their adoption of middle-class identities that will secure their hegemony into adulthood. It is rare to see the hero and bully settling their differences and becoming friends. Many suburban fantastic films simply restrict themselves to middle-class children and avoid any suggestion of other classes in their community. This perhaps reflects the simple reality of suburban life as an enclave in which children are segregated by class from birth. But it also reflects a gradual shift in representation, whereby the lower-middle- and middle-class families of suburban fantastic films of the 1980s (*E.T.*, *Back to the Future*) give way to the middle- and upper-middle-class families of the 1990s (*Home Alone*, *Jumanji*).

That said, suburban fantastic films generally identify with outcasts and the disadvantaged and persecuted. Usually this is manifest in the protagonist's sympathy for and sheltering of whatever element of the fantastic has entered suburbia (*E.T.*, *Gremlins*, *Harry and the Hendersons*, *The Iron Giant*). The protagonist's friendship and acceptance help heal the outcast's trauma of rejection and magically integrates them into a family or community. Suburban fantastic films teach the audience about compassion for others; in this, they are close to the animal or pet genre of family films. *The Goonies* is notable for the character of Sloth, (John Matuszak), a deformed brother of the crooks who is abused by them and ultimately befriends Chunk (Jeff Cohen), helps the kids against the crooks, and joins Chunk's family at the end. In *Mac & Me*, the main character Eric is paraplegic and his sympathetic representation (by Jade Calegory, an actor who is also paraplegic) is one of the few positive points of that film. *Explorers* even offers friendship across the class divide, when Darren (Jason Presson), a boy from the other side of the tracks befriends Ben (Ethan Hawke) and Wolfgang (River Phoenix) and he helps them construct the Thunder-Road spacecraft. However, the suburban fantastic's sympathy for the outcast has substantial limitations. Although some stories show genuine outcasts integrating into a community, suburban fantastic stories are generally about the sense of the white, male, middle-class child feeling outcast within a society that they feel they should otherwise dominate. Hegemony is usually prioritised over inclusion. White suburbia will accept anyone – as long as white, middle-class masculinity remains in charge.

The consequence of this focus on male pre-teens, then, is that a gender-neutral melodrama of maturation is inflected into a crisis experienced by the male protagonist about his identity. These films dramatise the moment in which a male character experiences an overwhelming existential anxiety about his impending patriarchal inheritance. The disruptive appearance of the element of the fantastic within suburbia symbolises the protagonist's new awareness of difficult and troublesome aspects of patriarchy, with which he needs to come to terms. Ultimately, his conflict with the fantastic reshapes his identity and retrofits his consciousness with the mentality that allows him to be a successful man. Although the parents have been mistrustful of him throughout the story, he is proved right in the end and they are forced to apologise to him. Bullies are defeated or get their comeuppance. The attractive girl-next-door is won through displays of daring and bravery. This is enough to create a happy ending of a maturation narrative, yet each film, to a greater or lesser extent, goes further than this. The character's whiteness, middle-class status, masculinity and heterosexuality are validated by subduing an all-encompassing, abstract Other, which is represented by the element of the fantastic, an heroic act which confirms the symbolic subordination of parents, female peers and other classes. The protagonist makes a compromise with patriarchy, accepting it in exchange for a heroism which flatter the male ego.

To indicate how typical this ending is, it is worth comparing it to the apocalyptic end of season seven of *Buffy the Vampire Slayer* (TV, 1997–2003) where we see for once a suburban fantastic protagonist refusing to accommodate patriarchal values, something only possible because the protagonist is female. Teenager Buffy (Sarah Michelle Gellar) spends seven seasons combatting demonic forces that emanate from a hellmouth underneath her suburb of Sunnydale. Ultimately, in order to defeat the demons of the hellmouth, Buffy symbolically shares her magical powers with all the young girls of the world, and this retrospectively recodes the demonic forces that she has been battling as the forces of patriarchy. The destruction of the element of the fantastic (the hellmouth under the suburb) symbolises the destruction of patriarchy. Rather than saving suburbia, Buffy and her friends destroy it totally. As such, *Buffy* completely and consciously inverts the usual conclusion of the suburban fantastic – the centralisation of power within the male protagonist, the subordination of femininity and the acceptance of a patriarchal task of perpetuating suburbia and its values.

*Between a Weaponised Robot and Nuclear Weapons*

The male-focus of suburban fantastic cinema doesn't just affect the forms of its melodrama. It also affects the kind of fantastic elements that intrude upon suburbia. Fantastic narratives focused on Frankenstein's monster, Pinocchio, Superman, male vampires and male-coded homunculi are adapted to reflect a male identity crisis.

For example, the Pinocchio story of an artificial, man-made boy who wants to become a real boy is updated in *D.A.R.Y.L.* where a boy (Barret Oliver) living with foster parents in the suburbs is revealed to be a robot prototype who has escaped from a scientific laboratory. Over the course of the story, Daryl is recaptured and returned to the lab where he was created. His creation has been financed by the military who are not interested in children who feel emotions, but in adult-sized soldiers and killing machines. Threatened with being destroyed, Daryl escapes with a scientist who has come to accept his humanity. Daryl ultimately fakes his own death and escapes to live a natural life as a permanently young boy in suburbia, fulfilling the scientist's dying assertion that 'you are a real boy, Daryl. You are a real boy.' The Pinocchio theme has been sounded and Daryl achieves a fantasy ending of perpetual childhood in suburbia with a loving family. But Daryl has not actually transformed into a real boy. Furthermore, nothing occurs in the narrative to prevent the construction of adult-sized soldiers. Daryl's fate, then, offers an apt symbol for the suburban fantastic's most extreme vision of socialisation: alienated from their own minds and bodies, pre-teens in suburbia are co-opted into a militarised, technologised world and are destined to grow up into militarised, technologised adults.

Other suburban fantastic stories also follow Pinocchio-style narratives where robots built as killing machines develop feelings and abandon the military for the pleasures of everyday life. In *Short Circuit*, the robot Johnny 5 (Tim Blaney) becomes sentient in a lightning storm and escapes from a military base into the surrounding area. Johnny is a stand-in for the usual pre-teen protagonist of suburban fantastic cinema. His emotional journey mirrors that of a child discovering the beauty of the world and the kindness of humans, yet Johnny 5 also discovers death when he crushes a grasshopper and learns the horrifying truth that he is a military weapon designed to kill. Like Daryl, he only survives by faking his own death and escaping to small town life where he can live 'off the grid'. In *The Iron Giant*, the

Giant undergoes a similar development. A superweapon built by an alien race that has accidentally crashed on earth, he befriends pre-teen Hogarth and through their friendship, they both discover the joys of friendship as well as the meaning of death (they see a deer killed). Gradually the Giant remembers that he is a superweapon built to kill, and, like Johnny 5, he renounces his intended purpose and choses to sacrifice himself in a nuclear explosion to save his friend and the town.

Although not literally pre-teen protagonists, these robot characters of Daryl, Johnny 5 and the Giant reflect the socialisation of pre-teen boys. They imply that pre-teen boys have been programmed with violent, militarised mindsets and this programming has turned them into gendered killing machines. However, they are capable of developing feelings and programming themselves, and this creates heroic endings where the protagonists are able to reset their programming toward more humane values and desires, even though their emotions always remain a consequence of their technological programming.

Other forms of the fantastic appearing in the suburban fantastic – Frankenstein's monster, Superman, male vampires, male-coded homunculi, and many others – require their own close assessment for the ways that they dramatise male socialization. However, the embodiment of the pre-teen protagonist as a militarised robot also reflects a more general association between pre-teen and teenage males and destructive, even apocalyptic, power. The Pinocchio narrative acknowledges that the idea of being an advanced military weapon capable of terrific destruction is an attractive fantasy to the audience, even as the films work through this fantasy and discard it in favour of more positive values. Indeed, suburban fantastic films repeatedly show the element of the fantastic sowing chaos and destruction, in the form of car accidents, fires, electrical short-outs, explosions and property damage, either across the suburb or located specifically in one home (*Poltergeist*, *E.T.*, *Gremlins*, *The Gate*, *The 'burbs*, *Jumanji*, *Small Soldiers*, *Zathura: A Space Adventure*, *Monster House*). The element of the fantastic is responsible for this destruction, but because of the connection between the main character and the element of the fantastic, it can be read as an expression of the protagonist's own feelings of frustration and antagonism towards suburbia.

Other suburban fantastic films express this destructive power of masculinity by associating the protagonists with nuclear weapons. For example,

David (Matthew Broderick) in *WarGames* comes very close to starting a nuclear war with Russia by tapping into a military mainframe from his bedroom and playing a computer game with Joshua, an advanced AI (named after a dead child of its creator) that thinks the game is real. Rob Latham notes that 'both David and Joshua are portrayed as lonely adolescents' (Latham 2002: 223) but that 'Joshua's playful spirit' is perverted 'toward literally genocidal applications' (Latham 2002: 230). Although David succeeds in averting nuclear war at the end, the destruction of the world is extremely high stakes for what is ultimately a teenager's socialisation. In *Jumanji*, only the prosperity of the town was at stake in the protagonist's choices, but in *WarGames* the survival of the whole world depends on the correct socialisation of the teenage protagonist. Although the reckless incompetence of David and the military almost ends the world, both are absolved of any blame by the happy ending.

*The Manhattan Project* offers a similar association in that the protagonist Paul (Christopher Collet) steals plutonium and makes a bomb at home to win a science fair and comes close to accidentally detonating it. Although he is acting in order to expose the risks of nuclear weapons, Paul is also recklessly attracted to its power. Even in *Weird Science*, when Gary and Wyatt try to show the bullies how they made their perfect woman Lisa, the wires end up touching a picture of a Pershing II ballistic missile, which suddenly erupts into the house through the floor. The 'magical' computer power they use to improve their social status and win the girls of their dreams is explicitly related to the danger of nuclear warheads. And less we forget, part of the premise of *Back to the Future* is that Marty is sent back in time while escaping from a group of Libyans from whom Doc Brown (Christopher Lloyd) has stolen plutonium to make the Delorean time machine.

These and other suburban fantastic films see a connection between the behaviour of talented teens and the technology of nuclear weaponry. On one level, these films are reflecting cultural anxieties about the abilities of a new generation of hyper-educated teens and the power they possess by having computers in their bedrooms. But they also use the image of nuclear weapons to express anxieties about the patriarchal power that young men are inheriting and whether they are going to wield that power responsibly. It may be flattering for pre-teen males to see their power presented as something which could destroy the world, but given the real-life existence of nuclear weapons, it is clear that suburban fantastic cinema allegorises, rather than exaggerates, the relation of masculinity and world destruction.

Some of the complexities of the relationship between pre-teen males and destruction and violence are neatly explored in the meta-referential suburban fantastic *Matinee*. In this film, set in 1962, Gene (Simon Felton) is new to the local high school of Key West, is struggling to fit in and is affected by his father's long absence with the navy. The story follows him settling into school and befriending Stan (Omri Katz). The two of them experience a series of adventures involving bullies and ultimately succeed in their respective advances on Sandra and Sherry. Their heroism is proved when Gene rescues his brother from a collapsing cinema balcony in front of Sandra and Stan stands up to Sherry's ex-boyfriend. In the final scene, Gene's personal anxieties are resolved by his father's safe return home.

This material could have furnished a traditionally nostalgic and senti-mental coming-of-age story. However, *Matinee* includes a unique historical frame. Gene's personal melodrama takes place in Key West during the Cuban Missile Crisis when the town has become populated by the army preparing for war. Gene is personally connected to this crisis because his father is serv-ing in the crisis. Gene is afraid for his father's safety and haunted by a dream where he imagines a nuclear bomb going off outside his front door.

Despite this fear, however, the prospect of world destruction is also vicariously enjoyed by Gene through his passion for cinema. Gene enjoys the new horror film 'Mant!' which portrays the effects of a scientific accident, turning a man into a giant ant (evoking the vein of 1950s horror films con-cerned with the effects of radioactivity from nuclear experimentation), and climaxes with a vision of a nuclear detonation. Gene is thrilled and terrified by this monster movie, just as he is thrilled and terrified by the presence of the army in the town. Gene's excitement is safely explored within cinema, but *Matinee* portrays a world in which such fantasies of destruction are actu-ally bringing the world to the brink of war. Carrying this thrill into real-world situations is terrifying, as evidenced by Gene's dream of a nuclear explosion. Gene, then, struggles to disentangle his feelings about destruction in the movies and real life through his personal relations. Gene wins a pacifist girl-friend Sandra, whose parents are proto-hippies and who is first encountered protesting duck and cover practice. Their relationship tempers his attraction to destruction and helps establish his masculinity and heterosexuality. However, Gene doesn't directly adopt her pacifist beliefs and the final shot

Gene (Simon Fenton) dreams a nuclear detonation in *Matinee* (1993).

is of his father's helicopter returning, an ambiguous image that mixes the relief of a parent returning safely with the anonymous threat of a returning military vehicle and the threat of conflict. Gene may have adopted a surface pacifism regarding war, but the pleasures of war and destruction have not been entirely renounced.

The male-focus of suburban fantastic cinema, then, works to implicate the pre-teen male protagonists in the destructive power of the element of the fantastic. Most suburban fantastic films downplay this implication and represent the fantastic as an external factor intruding into suburbia, rather than a projection of male desires and fantasies. However, the link between them is acknowledged directly in another film by *Matinee* director Joe Dante. In *The 'burbs*, three fathers and husbands, Ray (Tom Hanks), Art (Rick Ducommun) and Rumsfeld (Bruce Dern) suspect that their strange new neighbours the Klopeks are murdering people and start to investigate. However, the Klopeks are discovered to be innocent, and for a moment, the three white, middle-class adults are retrospectively reinterpreted by Ray as the 'weird' members of the street who are disrupting quiet suburbia.

> Ray: Remember what you were saying about people in the 'burbs, Art, people like Skip, people who mow their lawn for the 800th time, and then SNAP? WELL, THAT'S US. IT'S NOT THEM, THAT'S US. WE'RE the ones who are vaulting over the fences, and peeking in through people's windows. We're the ones who are THROWING GARBAGE IN THE STREET, AND LIGHTING FIRES. WE'RE THE ONES WHO ARE ACTING SUSPICIOUS AND PARANOID, ART. WE'RE THE LUNATICS. US. IT'S NOT THEM. It's us.

*The 'burbs* acknowledges the source of the fantastic disruption of suburbia within the paranoid anxieties of white, middle-class heterosexual American males. However, the film is ultimately ambiguous about how far it wants to condemn its main characters and in the last scenes, it reveals that the Klopeks *are* genuinely murderous and the protagonists are belatedly validated. Yet for a moment, *The 'burbs* acknowledges what is otherwise only implied in other suburban fantastic films: that the imaginations and neuroses of the white, male protagonists are the real source of the element of the fantastic, which is otherwise objectified into an external force that enters suburbia.

*Heroism and Superman*

In addition to affecting the kinds of melodrama and fantastic that appear in suburban fantastic movies, the focus on pre-teen and teenage males also affects the values promoted in the climax and conclusion. As previously mentioned, the process of maturation involves magically resolving all personal contradictions and adopting positive moral values of family, responsibility, duty, honour, trust, compassion, kindness and healthy forms of mutual attraction. These are certainly important values to promote to child viewers. Indeed, these films have been beloved by generations of children precisely because they acknowledge the audience's fears, hopes and dreams and offer comforting resolutions. But the promotion of such values is often accompanied by the promotion of a 'soft' patriarchy, meaning a normative heterosexuality, masculine hegemony, and a certain race and class status. These can be conveyed many ways depending on the nature of the melodrama, the element of the fantastic, and the specific values promoted. For each film, the final configuration of values is different.

For example, the moral value of peace is asserted in *Russkies*. Danny (Joaquin Phoenix), Adam (Peter Billingsley) and Jason (Stefan DeSalle), three boys living in Key West, have absorbed the jingoistic beliefs of their military fathers and their favourite comic book about a military hero named Sergeant Slammer. They discover a Russian soldier Mischa (Whip Hubley) washed up from a submarine and take him hostage. Their parents don't believe that they've captured a Russian and so the boys are left to gradually bond with him, and realise that he's just a young guy who wants an ordinary life like them. Together they enjoy the pleasures of an American lifestyle, going to baseball, go-karting and a parade. Ultimately, the boys decide to help him escape to Cuba and this leads to a tense stand-off in international waters between the Russians on the submarine and the American soldiers who have chased after Mischa and the boys. In the final encounter, Mischa saves Danny from drowning and Daddy's military father thanks Mischa and lets him go. The film then ends with the boys reading a comic book in which their hero Sergeant Slammer makes peace with his Russian enemy. Despite its militaristic setting, and its focus on three boys who are gung-ho at the prospect of World War III, *Russkies* is one of the most progressive suburban fantastic films in its attitude to the Cold War and the military. It shows the boys growing beyond the aggression and jingoism that they have absorbed from their surrounding culture and learning the virtue of compromise and accord with enemies. *Russkies* condemns American military hot-headedness and rehumanises the stock Russian villain.

In some suburban fantastic films, the most positive moral values are expressed through the male ideal of Superman. In the climax of *The Goonies*, Sloth pulls off his shirt, revealing a Superman shirt, accompanied by the theme music from the Richard Donner *Superman* movies, just before performing a daring feat. In *The Iron Giant*, Hogarth and the Giant bond over Superman comics and the Giant's final self-sacrifice is a conscious imitation of Superman. And in a more recent suburban fantastic, *Midnight Special* (Jeff Nichols, 2016), Alton (Jaeden Lieberher), an alien child with special powers, reads a Superman comic-book and identifies with him. Although Superman can be deployed in support of patriarchal hegemony and male saviour narratives, he also embodies benevolence, kindness and self-sacrifice, values that extend beyond patriarchy's narrow focus.

Occasionally, suburban fantastic films can end up promoting much more damaging forms of masculinity. In *Cloak and Dagger*, for instance, Davey is coping with his mother's death by obsessing about the Jack Flack spy agent franchise of video games and board games. When Davey uncovers an actual spy conspiracy involving secret plans hidden in a video game cartridge of Jack Flack, he ends up chased by spies in numerous dangerous escapades, accompanied by a fantasy projection of Jack Flack who appears beside him as a kind of guardian angel, giving him advice. His adventures end in a dramatic airport shootout where the enemy spies take Davey hostage onboard a plane with a bomb on it. Davey is saved because his father realises that Davey was telling the truth and boards the plane pretending to be the pilot. He rescues Davey, but when it explodes Davey horrifically believes that his father is dead. He survives however and walks out of the flames looking just like Jack Flack. In that moment, Davey realises that his father is a real-life hero and they are reconciled.

On the surface, *Cloak and Dagger* promotes a real father-son relationship over an imaginary fantasy of an impossibly ideal father figure. But looking closer, the choice between them appears false. Although Davey chooses his father at the end, his father's military background as a military air traffic controller and his bravery in the climax amalgamate Davey's father and Jack Flack together. Davey essentially gets to have both his father and his hero in one (emphasised by the same actor playing both roles). Although Davey's father makes the case for 'putting food on the table' and 'being around' as the real form of heroism, he ultimately proves himself through an act of daring worthy of Jack Flack himself.

Jack Flack, meanwhile, has revealed himself to be a dubious role model for young boys. Davey's internal Jack Flack has continually prompted Davey to react violently against the enemy spies. Indeed, at one point, Davey is cornered by an enemy spy and although Davey doesn't want to kill him, his internal Jack Flack tricks Davey into shooting the spy dead. Killing a man marks an important stage in Davey's maturation. Jack Flack says that Davey is 'growing up now' and so his fantasy projection of Jack Flack vanishes. By this, Davey appears to expel the violent tendencies which he has projected in the form of Jack Flack. However, Jack's voice continues to encourage Davey, and as with the fusion of his father with Jack Flack, it is clear a violent form of heroism is being validated. Davey, Davey's father and Jack Flack together form an ideal male trio of youthful pluck, fatherly care and military daring. Softening female influences are not required: Davey's mother is dead and his girl sidekick Kim is pre-pubescent and too young to be a love interest.

A similarly extreme promotion of male aggression as a positive virtue comes in *Watchers*, based on a novel by Dean Koontz. Pre-teen Travis (Corey Haim) is coping with his parents' divorce and the absence of his DELTA Force father. When he encounters a super-intelligent dog, he channels his father's DELTA Force abilities by setting booby traps to protect it from a corrupt government agent and a hybrid creature created in a government laboratory. Travis ends up killing both the hybrid creature *and* the corrupt government agent – all to save a dog and to overcome his personal grief at his family's separation. Travis's patriarchal fantasies of power, aggression and dominance are promoted under the guise of courage, duty and 'doing the right thing'.

*Cloak and Dagger* and *Watchers* are extreme instances of a general tendency to deliver patriarchal values under the guise of moral values. Few suburban fantastic films advocate for such negative versions of patriarchal values. Most suburban fantastic films emphasis soft patriarchal values of male domination, heteronormativity and class power, and intertwine them in complex ways with family, responsibility, duty, honour, trust, compassion, kindness and love.

## Conclusion

The male-focus of suburban fantastic cinema inflects the choice of both the melodramatic and the fantastic elements of the narrative, but they also affect its promotion of moral and ideological values. Suburban fantastic films emphasise a narrative of maturation where positive moral values are promoted and where the male protagonist saves his friends, family and town. But suburban fantastic films also complicate this by the constitutive link between the male protagonist and the element of the fantastic. Because of this, the element of the fantastic appears as a displacement of feelings that the male protagonist cannot otherwise express. In order to overcome their personal dilemmas and tame the element of the fantastic, the protagonist must adopt mature, adult leadership and responsibility. However, such 'ordinary' virtues are not sufficient to defeat the inflated threat of the element of the fantastic. In order to defeat it, the protagonist has to assume a heroic masculinity, which tacitly involves acquiescing in a 'soft' form of patriarchy (involving the reduction of female characters and working-class characters).

Nor is this socialisation limited to the protagonist. From the perspective of a heavily male heterosexual audience, it is this 'birth of a hero' narrative that provides the real attraction of suburban fantastic stories. Furthermore, the protagonist's experience – in which fundamental contradictions in their gender identity are symbolically resolved through a ritualised encounter with an external force – is duplicated in the experience of the suburban-dwelling audience finding symbolic resolution of their own contradictions and anxieties by watching suburban fantastic films. This audience is implicitly socialised into a soft patriarchal power that perpetuates male domination, as part of a larger socialisation described by Rob Latham: 'from early youth, boys and girls are tutored, through the image-based apparatuses of a self-serving and predatory system, in sexual objectification and the libidinal logic of master versus slave' (Latham 2002: 255). Although the perpetuation of male domination is a tacit theme of many mainstream male-focused Hollywood films, the emphasis on male pre-teens in suburban fantastic films that otherwise could be more gender-balanced, is notable.

# 4    MEDIA

In every suburban fantastic film, the element of the fantastic is a condensation of various invisible productive forces that are exerting a powerful influence on the characters and the world. Each suburban fantastic film offers multiple overlapping interpretations for the condensation taking place and understanding suburban fantastic cinema depends on adjudicating between the possible interpretations of the element of the fantastic in each film.

One of the most common interpretations traces the element of the fantastic into the media environment in which children are raised. The role of media images and narratives in socialising children is evident in society and is referenced within the suburban fantastic itself as an important, even defining, source of the element of the fantastic. Indeed, it is the introduction of television within middle-class suburban homes from the 1950s onwards that provides the real-life element of the fantastic that has invaded suburban living and which is alternately terrorising or attracting suburban residents, through its many images of other worlds and ways of life. The status of television in suburban living is acknowledged by the important background role of television in many suburban fantastic films. This can be observed if we look at a common trope in suburban fantastic films: a scene of television watching.

*The TV Watching Scene*

The syntactic connection between the male protagonist and the element of the fantastic – the defining condition of the suburban fantastic – is often indicated by a scene in which he watches television. This act of watching symbolically connects an instance of the fantastic (often a clip of a monster from a classic Hollywood horror movie) and the anxieties and imagination of the character. Although the protagonist watches a specific film clip, there is sometimes only a generic similarity between this clip (and the film it stands for) and the fantastic event that disturbs suburbia. This clip simply condenses a repertoire of popular figures and myths of contemporary culture familiar to children deriving from fairy tales, folk-tales, classic Hollywood B-movies, TV sci-fi and horror anthologies, pulp science fiction stories and classical literary predecessors. When an element of that larger repertoire appears in suburbia, it is as if it is the memory or imaginative externalisation or extension of what the character has seen on television. For example, in *E.T.*, the alien E.T. watches *This Island Earth*, a UFO invasion film that alludes to his appearance within Elliott's world. In *Gremlins*, Billy watches a scene from the original *Invasion of the Body Snatchers*, in which alien pods burst open. Immediately afterwards, when Billy falls asleep, his pet mogwai crystallise into pods and begin their metamorphosis into gremlins. In *The Goonies*, Sloth watches *Captain Blood* (Michael Curtiz, 1935), a pirate adventure with Errol Flynn, which indicates the general generic lineage of the film.

Further examples of characters watching old movies that have a bearing on the element of the fantastic that disrupts suburbia can be seen in *Explorers*, *D.A.R.Y.L.*, *Fright Night*, *My Science Project*, *The Manhattan Project*, *Invaders from Mars*, *Harry and the Hendersons*, *Pulse*, *Matinee*, *Small Soldiers*, *The Iron Giant* and others. The choice of film and film clip is particular to each suburban fantastic film and correlates specifically to the fantastic genre being pastiched. Hence, these televisual images are often directed more at the audience, as a generic indicator, than at the spectating protagonist.

The symbolic purpose of these scenes is to suggest a connection between the images introduced into suburbia through household television sets and the protagonist's imagination. Media images are socialising

Daryl (Barret Oliver) watches multiple television screens in *D.A.R.Y.L.* (1985).

the protagonist and the 'TV watching scene' stands in for his continual exposure to such images in the domestic environment. The intrusion of the element of the fantastic, then, appears implicitly as the product of the protagonist's mental recycling and repurposing of these media images to their own personal dilemmas. The film's use of pastiche is justified by the fact that children's behaviour is often a performative pastiche of adult behaviour, where they try on different adult 'styles', playing with them in a self-conscious way that conveys implicitly their interest in and attraction to these forms. The use of generic pastiches in suburban fantastic cinema, then, correlates with a real mental habit of pre-teens. And the scene of television watching allows suburban fantastic films to acknowledge cinematic and televisual images as the 'source' of the element of the fantastic.

The TV watching scene is supported by other indices of the importance of filmic and televisual media. Sometimes the protagonists have an interest in cinema itself (Data's (Ke Huy Quan) passion for James Bond in *The Goonies*, the consuming passion for Universal monsters of *The Monster Squad* and the kids' love of horror movies in *Matinee*) and this explicitly indicates the way that the protagonist's imagination is mediating between televisual images and the intrusion of the fantastic. Sometimes, posters for real films are displayed in the protagonists' bedrooms, clearly visible to the viewer. In *Poltergeist*, Carol-Anne and Robbie have a poster of *Alien* (Ridley Scott, 1979) in their bedroom. In *Gremlins*, Billy has posters of *Them!* and *Beginning of the End*. In *Russkies*, Danny has a *Commando*

(Mark L. Lester, 1985) poster in his room. In *Mac & Me*, in an interesting meta-referential touch, the poster above Eric's bed is of a TV before a child's bed. Such posters indicate generic ties between the featured films and the suburban fantastic film we are watching. But they also represent the kind of movies that have so colonised the minds of the protagonists that they have wanted to stick the poster up on their bedroom walls.

Indeed, the extent to which the events of the film mimic those that the protagonists have seen on television or cinema is acknowledged when the characters mention that the events of the film are the kind of thing that only happens in movies. For example, in *E.T.*, when Greg (K.C. Martel) suggests that E.T. just 'beam up' back to his spaceship (like the characters of *Star Trek*), Elliott looks at him scornfully and says 'This is reality, Greg.' Greg is chastised for presuming that any trope that he recalls from his televisual viewing now operates in his world. Elliott insists that there is still a clear distinction between movies and reality even if, in their world, with the appearance of the alien *E.T.*, the line has blurred somewhat. This exchange is important in that it reveals that the characters are harbouring the same sf tropes as the audience, that they live in the same world of references, except that for the characters, some of these references have taken real-life form. However, Elliott's insistence on the reality of his experience is unsettling, since it reminds the audience that what they are seeing is in fact *not* reality but precisely a movie of the kind that *E.T.* itself is trying to disavow in that moment. This gesture in *E.T.* is not as common in other suburban fantastic movies as the TV watching scene, but it highlights something that is operative in all of them: the complex referential layers through which these films are perceived, the dialogue between the audience's perception of their reality (which is already distorted by other media) and the film's representation of reality which reveals the living presence of cinematic and televisual tropes in their world.

*The Attitude Towards Television in Suburban Fantastic Cinema*

Suburban fantastic films connect the element of the fantastic to televisual media images broadcast into the home and co-opt television to cinema by making television the vehicle for delivering the power of movies. But they also reflect cinema's anxieties about the power and influence of television as a competing media form that can disrupt the pre-eminence of cinema.

Suburban fantastic cinema then displays contradictory and ambiguous attitudes towards television.

In *E.T.*, the representation of television is positively inflected because E.T. is a benevolent alien with a strong emotional bond to Elliott. We are offered an image of Elliott's sister Gerty watching *Sesame Street* (TV, 1969–) and E.T. subsequently learns the alphabet from the same show. By referring to programming which is intentionally designed to teach children, Spielberg highlights the educative and behavioural effect of television. This sense that behavioural programming can be experienced as a wonderful thing is strengthened in an earlier scene when E.T. watches *The Quiet Man* (John Ford, 1952) and simultaneously, through their shared psychic connection, inspires Elliott to imitate the actions on screen and kiss the pretty girl in his school class. The correlation between the representation of action on screen and its influence on the main character's behaviour perpetuates the idea that images, actions, behaviours and identities, viewed through the agency of television, influence the actions, behaviours and identities of pre-teen main characters. Furthermore, *E.T.* suggests that socialisation through media can be experienced positively, even ecstatically. The western iconography of *The Quiet Man* goes against the sf and horror images overwhelmingly prioritised by the suburban fantastic and indicates that Elliott is being conditioned into a kind of heroism and assertive masculinity that the film sees as beneficial.

In contrast to *E.T.: The Extra-Terrestrial*, *Poltergeist* offers a negative impression of the effect of television. This is evident in the night-time beginning when Carol-Anne is attracted to the television broadcasting dead air and hears voices behind the screen. Later, she is sucked into a vortex within her bedroom closet, and her voice is heard coming from the television as if she is trapped behind the screen. In *Poltergeist*, the white noise underlying all televisual broadcasting can literally consume children, a much more troubling representation of television's power than an old film influencing Elliott's behaviour. This beginning is also ironic since the American national anthem plays on the television before turning to white noise. This sets up a contrast between the entire ideological complex of America the nation, the flag and the anthem, and the anarchy and chaos of the poltergeist associated with the white noise, as if America and its contemporary cultural values are the real poltergeists communicating through corrupting media devices into the suburban home. At the end of

*Poltergeist*, the Freeling family move into a motel and eject the television set from their room, as if in a final repudiation of the source of all their problems. But the audience, perhaps watching *Poltergeist* on VHS, cannot escape as easily from the power of televisual images.

*Gremlins* shows both the positive and negative effects that television and movies are meant to have on children. In the climax, the gremlins gather in the local cinema to watch Disney's *Snow White and the Seven Dwarfs* (David Hand, 1937), a safe children's film that is explicitly focused on a virtuous role model for children. Yet by showing gremlins watching the film, rather than children, *Gremlins* implies that children are naturally anarchic and destructive, and that even watching a film like *Snow White* fails to inculcate positive values. Rather, the film encourages their anarchy and turns them into gremlins. Dante's film continually associates the gremlins with a force that has emerged from media images. When the gremlins see that Billy and Kate (Phoebe Cates) are trying to kill them in the cinema, the gremlins tear through the screen to reach them, as if they are themselves bursting through the boundary between movies and reality. And later in the department store, while Billy is chasing Stripe, the lead gremlin, Stripe appears on a bank of TVs for sale in the store. Thus, although the outbreak of gremlins is due to Billy irresponsibly breaking the three rules of looking after Gizmo, and is linked to his own personal frustrations, the outbreak is also a fantastic representation of the effect that cinema has on children. Tellingly, when Mr Wing (Keye Luke) returns to collect Gizmo, he criticises Billy for letting Gizmo watch TV, as if it were this that had led to the outbreak of gremlins.

Suburban fantastic cinema, then, shows television to be an ambiguous presence in the family home. Television can offer images that inculcate safe values for children (*Snow White*) or conventional ideas of heroism (*A Quiet Man*). But at the same time, television can deliver the terrifying white noise of *Poltergeist* or the anarchic spirit of *Gremlins*.

*Bursting Through the Screen*

Underlying both these representations of television is the idea that media images are conditioning their viewers, shaping their sense of reality, and also that media images can leave the screen and penetrate reality in some terrifying way. Indeed, this is a common theme within suburban

George McFly's reading appears to manifest in real life and inspires his later writing in *Back to the Future* (1985).

fantastic cinema. For example, *Back to the Future* acknowledges the effect of television and movies in a scene that obliquely alludes to the relationship between media images, a character's mind, and the element of the fantastic. In 1955, Marty's father George (Crispin Glover) dreams of writing sf stories, but his failure to ever stand up for himself leads him to abandon his ambition and by 1985 he has become addicted to television. *Back to the Future* seems to associate television with an inhibitive effect on individual industry and creativity. Yet other moments of *Back to the Future* testify to the transformative power of media images. In 1955, when Marty is trying to remasculinise his father by scaring him into action, Marty appears in his father's bedroom at night dressed in a radioactive protection suit and plays hard rock music to him through a pair of Walkman headphones, pretending to be 'Darth Vader', an alien from the planet Vulcan (humorously mashing *Star Wars* and *Star Trek* references for the audience). George glances at his comic book which has an image on the cover very similar to how Marty looks in his hamzat suit, and for a moment it seems to him as if the characters of his comic books have come alive in his bedroom. This is enough to scare George into seeking Marty's help into winning Lorraine. At the end of the film, the cover of his latest novel echoes the image of Marty in his 'Darth Vader' suit. The moment in 1955 when his imagination became real has implicitly led to this transformed reality and his own creativity. This chain of implications constitutes a brilliant pastiche of the premise of suburban fantastic cinema, that media images can have a transformative effect on an individual's life, if they are experienced as 'real'. Indeed, *Back to the Future* deploys this idea in the political realm as well. In 1955, Ronald Reagan is a minor movie actor, and Doc Brown reacts with incredulity that he might be president in the future. But in Marty's 1985, he and the audience know that Reagan's televisual media image has entered into the 'real world' in an uncanny form, as President of the USA.

This example from *Back to the Future* indicates the complex ways that suburban fantastic films can refer to the relationship between the protagonist, media images and the element of the fantastic. The nature of the relationship depends on the protagonist's personal dilemmas, the media images that they watch and the form of the fantastic. We can explore these variations in a handful of selected examples: *Explorers*, *The Monster Squad*, and *Matinee*. A conventional separation of movies from life is effected in *The Monster Squad*, while Joe Dante's two films show him once again subverting the conventions of the sub-genre in interesting ways.

*Case Study: Explorers (1985)*

In *Explorers*, Ben (Ethan Hawke) is latently dissatisfied with life. He lives with his mother and an unseen brother who is now in his 'jerk phase'. His father is never mentioned and he suffers from bullies at school and an impossible longing for a girl in his class. In reaction to this, he has absorbed himself in 1950s sf movies. His bedroom has a poster of *It Came From Outer Space* and he falls asleep watching *The War of the Worlds*. While asleep, he dreams of a circuit-board for a space-capsule. He manages to construct this as a vehicle dubbed 'The Thunder-Road' with two friends, Darren and a science nerd Wolfgang (River Phoenix) and they use it to travel into space. There they meet two aliens Wak and Neek who have been broadcasting the images of the circuit board to earth. Ben is told he received the message because he was 'special' and it is implied that his specialness comes from listening to his mother's advice that he should follow his dreams and make them a reality. Indeed, through his dream of the circuit-board, Ben achieves his dream of being an astronaut, of going into outer space and encountering alien life. When he first meets the aliens he says 'I've waited all my life to say this…. We come in peace'.

However, meeting the aliens is ultimately an ambiguous experience: 'This isn't how I thought it would be at all,' Ben says. The aliens turn out to be two 'kids' who have stolen their father's spaceship. They have also consumed so much human media, which has been spewing out from earth as transmission waves, that it affects their interactions. Wak, the male alien, does impressions of cartoons, chat shows, stand-up comedy and adverts. Neek, the female alien, is a parody of 50s female flirtatiousness. The aliens' personalities have been colonised by Earth's media to the extent that Ben finds interacting with them genuinely alienating. Yet what is really alienating to him is how they represent to Ben the way in which his own perspective on human society has been radically distorted by his own consumption of 1950s sf movies. Indeed, his dream of the Thunder-Road circuit-board is associated with a number of 'television watching' scenes of 1950s sf films like *The War of the Worlds* and *This Island Earth*. The Thunder-Road includes a TV screen as its main window, as if it is a giant mobile television set that the boys have managed to enter. And the interior of the alien spacecraft is an industrial maze of pipes and steaming vents suggesting a factory or production studio. Darren even finds an alien machine there capable of putting 'pictures in your head', which appears to be the source of Ben's dreams and an image of television broadcasting. The fact that the interior of the spacecraft evokes the dated alien space-ship interiors of films like *This Island Earth* also helps to establish the con-nection between Ben's fantasies and the element of the fantastic.

Ben tries to deny that television has such a distortive effect on people's minds by insisting on a clear separation between human reality and media:

> Ben: But this is just the movies. This isn't the way we really are. Don't you know that?
> Wak: You expect me to believe that. Look at this. Your people just like to blow things up. [...]
> Ben: But this isn't real. And we don't really kill people; well, we do, but not aliens, because we haven't met any.

Wak and Neek insist that movies show a particular human reality, a pro-pensity to violence that threatens them. Ben, by contrast, insists this is really fiction, even as he lives through an experience where his own media-inspired dreams have become real. *Explorers* accepts that such media-inspired dreams can become real but notes that not all media-inspired dreams are positive or desirable.

Ben's desires, then, remain unfulfilled by his encounter with media-tised aliens, but this disappointment is resolved by a shift in the relation between dreams and social reality. Wak and Neek give him a green crystal which appears to be able to make his dreams come true. Lori (Amanda Peterson), the object of his affections, now has dreams of the circuit board as well and when she sends him a note in class indicating that she knows about his trip into space, the crystal glows and leads Ben into a shared dream with her. They fly through the clouds and she kisses him, thereby resolving his masculine identity. It turns out that Ben's true desires have been to have a healthy human connection with a girl and the alien's magic crystal allows him to achieve this. However, despite the negative impact of intense television-viewing, his love of old sf movies is not abandoned. Wolfgang and Darren join this shared dream and plan to make a new advanced machine to travel into space again. Thus, after soberly warning against the dangers of television watching, *Explorers* ends by celebrating the powers of media.

*Case Study: The Monster Squad (1987)*

The opening scene of *The Monster Squad* depicts a European gothic castle, where the famous vampire hunter Van Helsing fights against Dracula but fails at the last moment to secure a complete victory. This fight is then resumed a hundred years later in the new location of American suburbia where the heroes are a group of pre-teen children led by Sean (Andre Gower). Sean's personal problems revolve around his parents' continual arguments about the father's workload at the police station. Sean takes refuge from this in his love of old Hollywood monsters and he is the leader of a monster movie appreciation club that meets in a treehouse. His sister Phoebe (Ashley Bank) is similarly affected by their parents' fights; however, she is rejected by Sean for membership to the Monster Squad and is generally afraid of monsters, so she takes comfort in Scraps, her dog soft toy. Both of their personal anxieties are brought to a crisis when the monsters from some of Sean's favourite movies – *Dracula* (Tod Browning, 1931), *Frankenstein* (1931), *The Mummy* (Karl Freund, 1932), *The Wolf Man* (George Waggner, 1941), and *The Creature from the Black Lagoon* (Jack Arnold, 1954) – gather in the town. Sean's cinema-watching obviously implies a connection between his fantasies and the emergence of the monsters. Dracula, his three demonic temptresses and his team of monsters constituted a dark vision of Sean's familial and social world. However, in contrast to other films where the monsters burst forth from the screen, *The Monster Squad* oddly shows that such monsters already exist in Sean's world. When Dracula gathers the monsters, he finds them in venues appropriate to their previous screen incarnations, as if Sean's real world is already saturated with cinematic landscapes and characters.

The monsters plan to find Van Helsing's diary and an amulet that can give them ultimate power, but Sean and his friends uncover this plot and work to prevent it. At the climax, this requires them to open a portal that pulls the monsters back into 'Limbo'. Defeating the monsters, then, does involve appropriately separating them from this world into another dimension and this also becomes the premise to resolve the family's conflicts. The father proves the value of his work by bravely confronting the monsters. Phoebe, having joined the Squad and overcome her fear of monsters by befriending Frankenstein, symbolically relinquishes her need for comfort by giving up her soft toy dog. And meanwhile, Sean has successfully led his friends on a mission to confront the monsters that he loves. The fact that he has to defeat characters that otherwise thrill him, acknowledges that they correlate with his feelings for his parents, whom he loves, even as their fights constitute the source of his anxiety. The movie ends with the family's bonds renewed and the restoration of the orderly masculine world. By the time the army turns up, the boys have already won and the film ends with Sean triumphantly asserting their communal identity as 'The Monster Squad' to the army commander, as if the military constitutes the only power that could validate this new identity.

Sean's family problems are resolved, then, but his relationship to cinema remains ambiguous. The fact that the monsters are relegated to another dimension at the end belatedly acknowledges that the monsters are not part of reality. The division between the real world and the cinematic world is re-established. But Sean remains fascinated with monsters. His love of horror films is validated in that his knowledge helped them defeat evil. And the deployment of these old familiar monsters has presumably renewed the group's affection for the films from which they derive. Such films are pure entertainment and Sean and his friends will continue watching monster films, even if they are not called up to fight them again.

*Case Study: Matinee (1993)*

One of the most explicit acknowledgements that the fantastic disruption is grounded in cinema images bursting off the screen into reality comes in a meta-referential suburban fantastic film, *Matinee*. We have already discussed Gene's personal melodrama, his relation to masculinity as embodied in the conflict between his pacifist girlfriend and his father's role in the Cuban Missile Crisis. But Gene has a passion for cinema and his life is disrupted by the premiere in the local cinema of director Laurence Woolsey's (John Goodman) new monster movie 'Mant!' (a Hollywood horror B-picture in which a man is turned into a giant ant), and the arrival in town of Woolsey to promote it. A William Castle-style director, Woolsey is not content with the audience's passive reception of the film. He pioneers the use of new technological devices and rigs the local cinema so that he can deliver extra-cinematic shocks to the audience (electric buzzers, actors running about in costume, a machine that simulates the experience of an earthquake). These devices project the effects of the movie into the real world of the auditorium, thereby making the audience part of the movie. Ultimately the devices malfunction, but the effect is so successful, it leads the audience to believe that a nuclear attack on screen is actually real, until they run out of the theatre and discover that their small town still exists.

Matinee uses this extension of the cinematic experience into the real world to comment upon the suburban fantastic's defining aspect – the intrusion of the element of the fantastic into reality. It shows that cinema itself lies behind the intrusion of the element of the fantastic into reality. It is the film director who is the real bogeyman, and what is really invading the town and provoking the fear of the protagonists are his images. The fact is that the element of the fantastic invading suburbia is in reality whatever latest must-see blockbuster is appearing this year in the cinema.

Films such as *Explorers*, *The Monster Squad* and *Matinee*, then, function as adult admonitions for children to clearly separate their sense of reality and fiction. They don't condemn the fact that movies influence the character's perception of the real world. But they acknowledge that movies can provoke a degree of reality-confusion in children. *The Monster Squad* shows a group of kids successfully separating their love of monsters from their sense of reality. But Joe Dante characteristically offers more subversive resolutions. In *Explorers*, movies and life remain entangled: the aliens themselves have been overwhelmed by the media images they have consumed. And in *Matinee*, cinema itself constitutes the element of the fantastic disrupting real life. Although Woolsey leaves the town, the presence of cinema in everyday life remains.

## Science and Technology

Although the connection between media images and the element of the fantastic is explicit, it's clear that television and cinema are simply the most common media technologies and forms that affect children's behaviour. Some suburban fantastic films identify other media and technologies as having a similar influence upon pre-teens and a connection to an intrusive fantastic force. For example, comic books both real and invented are important sources of influence in *Back to the Future, The Lost Boys, Russkies* and *The Iron Giant*. Rock'n'roll and heavy metal music is also an important influence, most notably in *Back to the Future, The Gate* and *Eerie, Indiana* (Episode 19, 'The Broken Record'). Perhaps the most significant purveyor of new media images at this time were home computers and video games. A set of films, with varying relations to the suburban fantastic – *Tron* (Steven Lisberger, 1982), *WarGames, Cloak and Dagger, The Last Starfighter, The Wizard* (Todd Holland, 1989) – imagine an element of the fantastic related to computers and video game worlds entering the lives of the protagonists. Suburban fantastic films generally prioritise film and television images over computer games, but protagonists of the suburban fantastic commonly have personal computers in their bedrooms, even in the early 1980s, and computers and computer imagery plays an important role in *WarGames, Cloak and Dagger, Explorers, Back to the Future, D.A.R.Y.L., Weird Science, Invaders from Mars, The Manhattan Project* and *Evolver*. Suburban fantastic films reflect anxieties over the increasing computerisation of society, from the computers in children's bedrooms (*D.A.R.Y.L.*) and video games (*Cloak and Dagger*), to the security of ATM machines (*Eerie, Indiana* (Episode 3, 'The ATM with the Heart of Gold')) and teenage hackers (*WarGames*).

The presence in suburban fantastic cinema of technologies that have an enormous influence on the lives of individuals living in suburbia, indicates that the connection between media images and the fantastic is underwritten by a specific historical and technological dispensation, i.e. the domestic presence of audio-visual technology (television, radio and telephone, VHS recorder, video camcorder, personal computer, walkie-talkie, and latterly internet and mobile phone). This technology can appear to have an almost magical power, attracting and repelling children and adults alike. Anxiety over this technology is expressed in numerous scenes in suburban fantastic cinema of domestic appliances malfunctioning and taking on a life of their own (*Poltergeist, Gremlins, Making Contact, Poltergeist II, Pulse*). *Gremlins* is the most direct in acknowledging this by linking the appearance of the gremlins to technology. Their antics often involve making domestic appliances and machinery malfunction, with Mr Futterman (Dick Miller) insisting that foreign manufacturers put gremlins in machinery. Billy's father Mr Pelzer (Hoyt Axton), in his summarising voice-over at the end of the film, supports this interpretation:

Well, that's the story. So, if your air conditioner goes on the fritz or your washing machine blows up or your video recorder conks out... Before you call the repairman turn on all the lights, check all the closets and cupboards, look under all the beds, 'cause you never can tell – there just might be a gremlin in your house.

The film has already linked the appearance of the gremlins to a number of different sources such as a mysterious shop in Chinatown, Billy's imagination and frustrations with his life, and cinema itself. But the conclusion stresses this connection with the dangers of technology in general, suggesting that it is not just cinematic technology that is of concern, but the whole technological regime in which suburbia is enmeshed.

This technological regime does not end at the limits of suburbia. Domestic technology relies on energy networks that have their origin far beyond the boundaries of suburbia. The electrical discharges that are common when technology malfunctions in suburban fantastic films indicates that the larger power of electricity and energy itself stands behind the uncanny behaviour of domestic technology. Through common imagery of pylons, electrical substations and phone lines, the audience is made aware of a largely invisible electrical network that connect the home and small town to the 'grid'. This is addressed directly in *Pulse*, where the electricity coming into David's (Joey Lawrence) house is possessed by some supernatural force. The electricity makes appliances come alive spontaneously in the house and appears to harbour some mysterious malevolence towards the residents. Ultimately David and his father (Cliff de Young) trap the malevolent force in the electrical circuits of the house and it is apparently killed there when the electricity pole falls on the house and makes all the electrical circuits in the house explode. But in the final scene the wall clock of the boy next door is pulsing with electricity, suggesting that the malevolent force has survived and will continue to plague suburban residents.

It is clear that the suburban fantastic reflects anxieties about the influence of technology in general and mass popular culture as a whole, rather than just the influence of television and televisual images alone. Television and its broadcasts are the vehicles through which a general unease about how inanimate technological objects can 'come alive' through the power of electricity is represented. This is the real-world anxiety that was also reflected in the situation of the child-protagonist's toys coming alive. Although few suburban fantastic films trace the source of the element of the fantastic all the way into the electricity grid and the uncanny nature of power and energy that suburbia relies on, many suburban fantastic films allude to these sources through two common tropes.

Firstly, the protagonist of suburban fantastic cinema is often put in a close relationship to science. Either they themselves are budding scientists and engineers who perform experiments and go beyond conventional adult science (Data in *The Goonies*, Gary and Wyatt in *Weird Science*) or they have a relationship to a crackpot inventor (Doc Brown in *Back to the Future*, Wolfgang in *Explorers*, Mr Peltzer in *Gremlins*, Wayne Szalinski (Rick Moranis) in *Honey, I Shrunk the Kids*, Edgar Teller (Francis Guinan) in *Eerie, Indiana*, Lawrence Woolsey in *Matinee*, and so on). Occasionally these figures combine to create protagonists who are technological or scientific prodigies (David Lightman in *WarGames*, Michael Harlan (John Stockwell) in *My Science Project*, Paul (Matthew Laborteaux) in *Deadly Friend*, Paul in *The Manhattan Project*). Such social types are only possible because real life suburban spaces have become technologised to such a high degree. For pre-teens, the figure of the adult 'genius scientist' appears to stand for an idealised vision of objective, unemotional masculinity, an emblem for what all the protagonists of suburban fantastic cinema should grow up into. However, the image of the pre-teen science genius is even more desirable, and, indeed, the adult crackpot inventors in suburban fantastic cinema retain an undisciplined eccentricity that smacks of childhood. By being joined with the youthful protagonist, the science genius becomes the figure of an individual perfectly attuned to the technological society they are starting to join.

Immanuel Wallerstein suggests why these films select the science genius as their idealised form of male maturity when he states that 'Scientific culture [has become] the fraternal code of the world's accumulators of capital' (Wallerstein 2011: 84). The positive representation, then, of the pre-teen science genius is a fantasy image of successful capitalists, who use reason and science to support continued capital accumulation. Suburban fantastic cinema isn't encouraging its audience to become scientists as such but is idealising adult work with the glamour of science. According to Fredric Jameson, the scientist is a 'distorted reflection of our own feelings and dreams about *work* alienated and unalienated: it is a wish-fulfillment that

The military-industrial complex in *WarGames* (1983).

takes as its object a vision of ideal [...] work' (Jameson 1971: 405; see also Frayling 2006). The protagonist's triumph over the fantastic is the triumph of their reason and problem-solving abilities, both of which help initiate the pre-teen protagonist into socially-approved adulthood.

Secondly, the otherwise obscured source of power and energy (power stations, technological manufacturers, as well as Hollywood as the producer of images) is manifest in the military installations, research laboratories and technological institutes (*D.A.R.Y.L.*, *Invaders from Mars*, *Russkies*, *Matinee*, *Small Soldiers*) that exist on the borders of suburbia and are implicated in the fantastical disruption. During the crisis of the story, these institutes typically send agents into the suburb in order to interrupt the protagonist's adventure with their own nefarious agenda. Their purpose is to control the element of the fantastic and harness it to their own ends, often by exploiting it in damaging ways.

Indeed, the fantastic element itself is always complexly imbricated with science, as it most often appears as a form of science fantasy. Even if the fantastic event can be plausibly based in science, it is still supplemented by supernatural or occult aspects. For example, in *E.T.*, the alien E.T. is scientifically plausible to a degree, and is revealed to be a scientist, able to construct telecommunication equipment; at the same time E.T. has magical healing powers and returns from the dead. Similarly, even if the fantastic is clearly supernatural, it is inflected with a scientific dimension: in *Poltergeist*, paranormal experts use the latest technological devices to test the house for a ghost, and the ghost itself is connected to the television set and electricity. Science fantasy is, in fact, the most common form taken by the element of the fantastic because it reflects the disposition of pre-teens, for whom magic no longer exists, but for whom clearly many implausible things are turning out to be true. They are attracted to science as a way of distinguishing plausible and implausible possibilities and their encounter with the fantastic represents an encounter with the most implausible (i.e. fantastic) possibilities of science.

The way the protagonist defeats the element of the fantastic and the agents that wish to control it, is critical to our final understanding of the element of the fantastic in any suburban fantastic film. But even when the narrative is in the form of the 'science experiment gone wrong', scientific or technical know-how is used to resolve the consequences, and it is the fantastic element that is dismissed and not science itself. Science then stands both as the invisible force producing the element of the fantastic and the body of knowledge that the protagonist draws on to solve the element of the fantastic.

*Conclusion*

Although the link between the main character's personal melodramas and the intrusion of the element of the fantastic prioritises the main character's personal anxieties as the 'source' of the fantastic, it is clear that their anxieties also reflect a larger common anxiety about the 'fantastic' power and possibilities of science and technology. Electrical energy and invisible broadcast signals enter suburbia and animate all the domestic technology of the home, including pre-eminently the television which delivers the images of Hollywood. As we have seen, these images stand in for a modern media informational and communicational environment which is colonising the imaginations of the protagonists and influencing their fantasies. And the elements of the fantastic that subsequently appear are connected to these images. Suburban fantastic cinema reflects real social anxieties about the influence of media on children's development and their early exposure to violence, sex and swearing through television and film. But those TV images, and the element of the fantastic which they anticipate, are also mystified expressions of that material technological infrastructure that extends into suburbia and influences it fundamentally, even though it is largely invisible. This is acknowledged in certain suburban satires (that is, not suburban fantastic, by our definition) which represent situations in which the entire terrain of suburbia has becomes a media image through the technology of television production. Films like *Stay Tuned* (Peter Hyams, 1993) and *Pleasantville*, in which the suburban protagonists are sucked into their television, and *The Truman Show* (Peter Weir, 1999), in which the suburban protagonist slowly realises that he is living in a continuous live TV show, take this idea to its logical limit. *The Truman Show* presents Truman Burbank (Jim Carrey) who discovers that his whole suburban life is actually a TV show and everyone around him is an actor. Suburbia is depicted as a panopticon, a place where the individual is a corporate product and is almost totally controlled by media, advertising and internalised behaviour patterns. Although the narrative shows Truman rebelling against the constraints of his town and ultimately breaking free of the TV show, its final shots turn Truman's situation back onto the audience, by showing the audience failing to break free of the television's control. Instead of turning off, they turn over to something else to feed their addiction to television. *The Truman Show* reveals what is usually only implied in the suburban fantastic: that the 'natural' space of suburbia has been invaded by a technological media apparatus and infrastructure to such an extent that pre-teen suburban residents are on some level as co-opted and colonised by the media as Truman.

# 5   MULTINATIONAL CAPITAL

So far, we have connected the various elements of the fantastic that intrude into suburbia to the protagonist's identity crisis regarding their relation to patriarchal power and their exposure to televisual and media images through domestic technology. However, there is one other productive force condensed in the element of the fantastic in suburban fantastic cinema. This is the force of multinational capital.

Multinational capital is clearly involved in the patriarchal power and the televisual images that are otherwise positioned as sources of the fantastic. By triumphing in the contest with the fantastic, the pre-teen protagonist claims their heroic identity and accepts a 'soft' form of patriarchy, manifest as social, gender and class hegemony while simultaneously disavowing or looking past the 'harder' aspects of patriarchy (violence, aggression). Furthermore, they subordinate the influence of fantastic televisual imagery to the realities of mature social relations without entirely rejecting television, media and science. What remains unaddressed in both these compromises is the force of multinational capital that promotes patriarchy and produces such televisual imagery in the first place. Usually, it is incarnated as distant 'villainous' figures employed in political, military and corporate institutions, which threaten the protagonists and are ambiguously linked to the element of the fantastic. When the intrusion of the fantastic is resolved, the institutions are also symbolically defeated. But the force of multinational capital is almost never directly confronted and defeated within the narrative; it remains in the background as a problematic aspect of the protagonist's reality.

## Government, Military and Scientific Forces

We can observe these multinational forces manifested in different forms within suburban fantastic films. For example, in *E.T.*, E.T. is left behind because the peaceful aliens gathering botanical specimen are disturbed by sinister government scientists, who appear intent upon capturing one of them. Suspecting that one has been left behind, they go on to eavesdrop on the families living in the suburb. Whenever they are seen investigating, their faces are obscured, they speak in muffled tones, and move in a group, projecting light from their torches. Their leader is represented by the keys that hangs at his belt and his face is unseen, indicating the anonymous and inhuman forces that he represents. These governmental scientists introduce a second fantastical world into *E.T.* after the aliens themselves. By showing government agents spying on suburban residents, *E.T.* encourages paranoia about the intentions and technological capabilities of government. They are not a realistic presentation of corporate or governmental forces. They are just as phantasmatic as the alien

Government agents invade domestic space in *E.T.: The Extra-Terrestrial* (1982).

forces, an aspect strongly presented in the scene where Elliott's house is invaded by government agents dressed in NASA spacesuits; they appear as disturbing and invasive as the alien they are hunting.

Following, *E.T.*, federal agents (FBI or CIA), military commanders and government scientists who are either responsible for creating the intruding element of the fantastic or who are attempting to contain and control the element of the fantastic for their own ends, all become important antagonists in suburban fantastic cinema. Such governmental, scientific or military forces turn up in *D.A.R.Y.L., Making Contact, Short Circuit, Flight of the Navigator, Mac & Me* and others, and tend to have standardised representations. Military figures are signified by anonymising camouflage, military scientists are signified by generic 'white coats' and clipboards, and federal figures tend to be identically suited and convey impassive expressions from behind sunglasses. According to Fredric Jameson, this anonymity is a sign of the multinational capital that is producing such government and military and scientific figures. Referring to the genesis of this figure in the 1970s conspiracy thriller, Jameson writes that:

> the FBI agent ... comes to occupy the place of that immense and decentralized power network which marks the present multinational stage of monopoly capitalism. The very absence in his features becomes a sign and an expression of the presence/absence of corporate power in our daily lives, all-shaping and omnipotent and yet rarely accessible in figurable terms, in the representable form of individual actors or agents. (Jameson 2011: 69)

Thus, in the FBI agent, 'capitalism becomes objectified and dramatized as an actor and as a subject of history' (Jameson 2011: 71). This marks something of a reversal in the use of passive anonymity, since in 50s sf, this iconography was used to connote both an alien doppelganger and communist sympathiser (cf. *Invasion of the Body Snatchers, Invaders from Mars*), figures that the main characters were confronting in the name of small-town American values. By the time of suburban fantastic cinema in the 1980s, it is the American federal and corporate world that has become a sinister agent disrupting suburban life. Suburban fantastic cinema marks out the retreat of any sense of genuine communist danger within suburbia, and the advance of a new invasive capitalism.

This force affects the family as well, since the protagonist's parents, particularly their fathers, can find themselves advocating for the authority of these governmental, scientific and military figures against the interests and beliefs of their own children (*Cloak and Dagger, Invaders from Mars, The Lost Boys, Russkies*). In doing so, they take on some of the sinister emptiness and automatism of FBI agents. By co-opting parents to champion multinational capital under the guise of the values of law and order, the protagonists are faced with the most challenging part of their struggle, yet by fighting against it, they liberate their parents who ultimately thank them for waking them up to the malevolence of the authorities. The protagonists thereby secure the parents as a protective cover for them from the multinational forces arranged against them.

The final judgment on these antagonistic forces is different for each suburban fantastic film. Representations of sheriffs and local law enforcement can be more sympathetic and humanising (*Jumanji*). And it is always possible that figures in authority will ultimately have a change of heart and join the hero in the end. For example, *E.T.*'s attitude to the government scientists is ultimately tempered. After the scientists invade Elliott's home and capture E.T., the leader's face (and, correspondingly, his humanity) is revealed. He and his team work to save E.T. from his sickness, rather than conducting experiments on him or letting him die. And although the government do try to stop E.T. and Elliott escaping to the forest at the end, the leader actually works with Elliott's mother to find the kids and doesn't stop E.T. from leaving. *E.T.* thus incorporates even the government scientist into its community of wonder at the end. Other examples of antagonists integrated into the 'community of wonder' include those in Charlie Drake (Dick Miller) in *Explorers*, Jacques LaFleur (David Suchet) in *Harry and the Hendersons*, and Dr Ellen Lamb (Kathryn Walker) in *D.A.R.Y.L.*. In general, it is easier to be integrated into this community if the antagonist lacks a financial or institutional motivation (Charlie Drake is a helicopter pilot, LaFleur is an independent hunter). Few suburban fantastic films are willing to reconcile antagonistic governmental or military forces to the heroes. Even *E.T.*'s reconciliation with the government scientist is only partial and symbolic. The other government scientists presumably remain dedicated to their mission to capture and experiment upon any aliens that are unlucky enough to land on earth and not find shelter with someone like Elliott. E.T. may escape, but Spielberg's film never entirely confronts or defeats these federal, military and scientific forces.

*Corporate Forces in the Suburbia*

Multinational capital also manifests itself in the representation of the corporate business world, or, more specifically, the force that produces the commodities that clutter suburbia. From this perspective, the protagonist's encounter with the element of the fantastic is really an encounter with the mystical power of commodities and it resolves their identity crisis not just towards a conventional heroic masculinity but towards being a consumer.

For example, early suburban fantastic films clearly establish the protagonists as consumers of the *Star Wars* brand. *Star Wars* had laid the ground for the suburban fantastic audience by establishing the reign of a kid's-oriented modern blockbuster at the box office and a shift towards special effect extravaganzas in the sf, horror and fantasy genres. But *Star Wars* was also one of the most infamous instances of a film capitalising on its success with merchandise. George Lucas's retention of the merchandising rights of *Star Wars* allowed him to exploit an enormous market for *Star Wars*-branded children's toys and clothes. Starting with both *Poltergeist* and *E.T.*, and continuing with *Gremlins, Red Dawn, Back to the Future, Explorers, Making Contact, My Science Project, Invaders from Mars* and many others, *Star Wars* appears through dialogue references and bedroom set props and costumes, indicating that these protagonists are consumers living in commercialised environments of franchise branding.

The mystical power of commodities, their ability to attract consumers and be consumed, is allegorised in the protagonist's struggle with the element of the fantastic. As we have already seen, the fantastic is often identified with a particular object that contains a fantastic energy or power (television, board-game, etc.). The protagonist's task becomes that of taming the power of the commodity so that it doesn't overwhelm them or their reality. This struggle is necessary since in the world of the suburban fantastic, commodities are starting to dominate the world of the protagonists. *Star Wars* is just one brand within a generally commercialised environment. *E.T.* prominently featured 'Dungeons & Dragons', *Sesame Street*, 'Speak and Spell' electronic toys, pincher/grabber wands, *The Incredible Hulk*-branded merchandise, and famously gave a commercial boost to Reese's Pieces. As Vivian Sobchack says, 'the suburban bedroom stuffed with toys and emblazoned with commercial logos figures as a microcosm

Shameless product placement of McDonalds Restaurants in *Mac & Me* (1988).

of contemporary consumer culture in its "purest form"' (Sobchack 1997: 245). Subsequent suburban fantastic films exhibited more overt product placement. In *Flight of the Navigator*, David (Joey Cramer) is given 'G.I. Joe' and 'Transformers' toys when he stays at a NASA base. In *The Monster Squad*, Eugene (Michael Faustino) wears 'Robotech' pyjamas. And in one infamous scene, *Mac & Me* pauses the dramatic action in order to heavily promote McDonalds restaurants. Such overt product placement fades in the 1990s when suburban fantastic cinema fuses with family films. *Jurassic Park* offers a self-conscious reminder of the audience's exposure to product placement in a scene in which the camera pans along a shelf stocked with merchandise branded for the resort, merchandise which the audience would also be able to purchase in the 'real' world. But arguably, in films like *Casper* and *Toy Story*, product placement has consolidated around the suburban lifestyle itself and the movie's own merchandise, rather than the products of other companies (see Lehu 2008).

This product placement is significant because it indicates that the protagonists are living in the same worlds of merchandise and branding as the audience. By depicting real products within the domestic environments of suburban fantastic films, such films draw a strong connection between these environments and those in which the audience actually lives. The audience can purchase the very same toys they see the protagonists play with. Allusions to *Star Wars* and other real-life films through bedroom posters and clips advertise these products to the audience at the same time as performing other functions like verisimilitude, character development and genre association. Indeed, suburban fantastic films are opportunities to create a market for entirely new merchandise. Thus, we find characters, vehicles and devices that originate in suburban fantastic films becoming soft toys, action figures and toy cars. This is perhaps little different from the merchandising strategies of other popular genres, but by portraying the consumers of such products, in the domestic space in which such products are consumed, suburban fantastic films reflect upon the process of consumption. They acknowledge that the audience, like the protagonist, is already living in a deeply commercialised environment, and that they themselves are both products to be consumed, and consumers of products (see Latham 2002). The protagonist represents the audience of modern Hollywood blockbusters such as *Star Wars*, and suburban fantastic narratives allegorise the encounter of the protagonist with products and merchandise, particularly those of Hollywood.

We can see this acknowledged in Joe Dante's *Small Soldiers*, one of the most satirical suburban fantastic films. In it, a toy manufacturer is taken over by a global conglomerate, one with a military division. They insert an advanced military computer processor into a new set of toy soldiers, the Commando Elite. This chip gives the toys a limited sentience to carry out their programmed mission of destroying a line of toys called the Gorgonites, a peace-loving set of bizarre creatures designed before the corporate take-over as educational toys for children but now repurposed as enemies of the Commando Elite. Unfortunately, once the Commando Elite are turned on, they are so intent on the violent destruction of the Gorgonites, they end up pursuing them through the suburban town to the homes of Alan (Gregory Smith) and Christy (Kirsten Dunst), where they besiege them and their parents. The chips in the toys can only be destroyed by a nuclear blast and Alan manages to simulate one when he climbs an electricity pole and sets off a small scale EMP pulse that destroys the computer processors of the Commando Elite.

The intrusion of the fantastic into the suburban environment is then, on one level, the product of a shift within global culture, where a small toy manufacturer making educational toys is taken over by a multinational conglomerate with a military division. The pressure to make a toy that sells

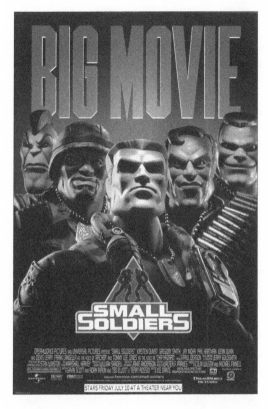

The poster for *Small Soldiers* (1998).

prompts the manufacturers to cut corners and put out a product without testing it beforehand. And the toys themselves are clearly designed to sell military values and violence to children under the guise of 'action'. Yet this is a process that the audience themselves are subject to, even with this very film. *Small Soldiers* put the military soldiers front and centre of its marketing campaign and even licensed a series of military toys to promote the film. The extent to which *Small Soldiers* itself is an advert for a toy line is acknowledged in the film when the head of Globotech, the toy's manufacturer, surveys the suburban carnage created by his products and laments the destruction by saying 'It's too bad. This would have been a hell of a commercial!', a satirical comment that rebounds intentionally on the film itself.

Nevertheless, the satire of *Small Soldiers* works because it relies upon the fact – clear to all children – that *Small Soldiers* is a commercial for militarised toys that promote violence as action, and that it is the audience's own desire for violent action, for toys and for exciting films that is permitting such a commercialisation of cinema. The audience has a guilty awareness that they are as susceptible to these forces as the film thinks they are – that's why they're currently watching *Small Soldiers*, a film in which a boy who is susceptible to over-commercialised toys, learns of their dangers and ultimately returns to the healthier toys of the Gorgonites. Multinational and increasingly global corporations socialise children through marketing commodities to them, and suburban fantastic cinema reflects this implicitly in representing an encounter between a consumer and a fantastic commodity that can be purchased from toy shops, after the screening is over.

*Natural Forces*

Suburban fantastic films in which powerful multinational forces are commercialising the environment of the protagonist can be usefully contrasted with those films that view suburbia and small towns as 'natural' environments free from hyper-commercialisation, places that are rooted in the deep rhythms of contemporary everyday life and the values of friendship, family and happiness. *Gremlins* begins with snowy images of Kingston Falls with happy Christmas music and kids throwing snowballs. The use of local radio sounds establishes an acceptable level of small-town commercialisation. Films that feature Christmas, like *Home Alone* and *Jumanji*, or that take place at Halloween, like *E.T.* and *Hocus Pocus*, draw upon the social rituals and folk culture of family life.

*The Sandlot* offers an almost comprehensive presentation of the rhythms of suburban life in 1962 – the summer rituals of baseball, town fairs, relaxing at the swimming pool, barbeques on the Fourth of July, and assorted minor scrapes. This 'timeless' rhythm implicitly underlies all representations of suburbia in the suburban fantastic and is indicated through establishing overviews of the normalcy of the suburban setting, for example, the images of the Cuesta Verde suburban estate at the start of *Poltergeist*. The protagonist might have their own dissatisfactions with life there, but it is clear that for other children suburbia is an attractive, even utopian, place, in which they can run wild with the pleasures of childhood

– friendship, first love, the freedom of riding a bicycle, passion projects such as sport or building bases or camping in nature, summer holidays and childhood festivals, such as birthdays, Halloween and Christmas.

Within this environment, the representation of the element of the fantastic also becomes radically naturalised. For example, in *The Sandlot*, the element of the fantastic is manifest in a fearsome dog owned by a scary old man, Mr Mertle (James Earl Jones). Pre-teens Scotty (Tom Guiry) and Benny (Mike Vitar) lose their baseball on the side of the fence where the dog lives and the elaborate mechanical devices they construct to recover their ball increasingly push the story into the realm of the fantastic. At one point, the dog appears in silhouette as a dinosaur, symbolising the boys' inflated fear of it, but by the end, the dog and Mr Mertle are acknowledged to be friendly and kind at heart. Confronting the dog and old man allows Scotty and Benny to overcome their feelings of fear and inadequacy and realise the essential harmlessness of their 'animal' masculinity.

*Stand by Me* (Rob Reiner, 1986) also provides a naturalistic version of suburbia and the fantastic. Set in 1959, it follows four boys, Gordie (Will Wheaton), Chris (River Phoenix), Teddy (Corey Feldman) and Vern (Jerry O'Connell) growing up on the fringes of the the small (fictional) town of Castle Rock, Oregon. By largely ignoring the prevailing media environment of the kids and substituting the iconography of the pristine suburban streets for older, pre-suburban domestic dwellings, *Stand by Me* represents a moment just before the standardisation of childhood by suburbia and by media. Correspondingly, their encounter with the fantastic is naturalised as well. Following a rumour, they dare themselves to trek into the forest to find a dead body. This journey and their eventual bravery in looking at the body turns the element of the fantastic into merely the unaccountable presence of death within life.

Both *The Sandlot* and *Stand by Me* also expand their naturalised elements of the fantastic into the narrative frame. *Stand by Me* begins with the adult Gordie (Richard Dreyfus) hearing that his old friend Chris has died and reflecting back on the summer when they went to find the dead body. Thus, their journey as pre-teens in 1959 is paralleled by their subsequent journey through time into adulthood and the present. The boys are not just discovering the reality of death; their journey into the forest allegorises the course of their own lives, and the death they discover at the end is really a confrontation with the reality that they themselves will one day die. Similarly, *The Sandlot* is framed with the perspective of Scotty after he has grown up (played by David Mickey Evans, the director). By meeting the feared Mr Mertle, Scotty and Benny learn that they are similar to him in that he also loves baseball. However, being old, he also represents the truth that time passes and that they will not always be young boys. This theme is strengthened at the end, when adult Scotty's voice-over nostalgically acknowledges that years have passed since the events depicted in 1962 and the protagonists have already grown into adults. Benny has become a decent baseball player, fulfilling his dream and Scotty is a commentator, still idolising him. *The Sandlot* has a more positive sense of the future possibilities for the boys than *Stand by Me*. Rather than death, it emphasises that time itself is the element of the fantastic entering their lives. Meeting Mr Mertle helped them accept that they are also part of a temporal process and not to fear the effects of time and aging.

Both *The Sandlot* and *Stand by Me* are liminal entries into the suburban fantastic sub-genre, since by naturalising the fantastic into the procession of time and the reality of death, they complicate the protagonist's heroic overcoming of the fantastic element. But both films serve to emphasise the fact that suburban fantastic films usually navigate between these two naturalising and commercialising tendencies, just as they navigate between depicting processes of 'natural' maturation and ideological socialisation. Films like *Mac & Me* and *Small Soldiers* envision suburbia and the fantastic to be dominated by commercialisation, in the production of consumers and the marketing of products. But usually, the effect of commodification and multinational capital are intertwined in complex ways with the knowledge of death and the passing of time, and condensed in the element of the fantastic that disrupts the timelessness of childhood.

## Property Development

The corporate and commercialising forces in suburban fantastic cinema find their most significant expression in the representation of property development. The suburb may be generally represented as a 'natural' area safe from commercialising forces. But when those commercialising forces are property developers, it becomes clear that the suburb is never a 'natural' area. Property developers constitute a productive force that is ultimately responsible for the construction of the suburb. Suburbia is not just the scene of increasing commodification, it is also a commodity itself to be produced and consumed. The struggle between the protagonists and property developers can appear to lead to a victory against these commercialising forces. However, as usual, victory masks a compromise: the protagonists can never fully defeat the multinational capital exploiting their 'natural' environment.

For example, *Poltergeist* implies that the suburb itself can ultimately be interpreted as the element of the fantastic that is intruding upon the protagonists' lives. It does this by linking the construction of the suburb to the presence of the poltergeist. The Freeling family's home is haunted by ghosts apparently because property developers built the Cuesta Verde estate over a cemetery without relocating the bodies. Thus, it is the very foundation of the suburb established by a property development company that motivates the poltergeist's disruption of the Freeling home. The commercial appropriation of sacred land is a crime that has cursed Cuesta Verde and its occupants. One might expect the Freeling family to ally themselves with the poltergeist, to shame the property developers and end up remaining in suburbia reconciled with the poltergeist. However, the heroes and villains are more closely identified than in other suburban fantastic films. The Freelings are marked out as being appropriate victims of terror. Although Steven Freeling (Craig T. Nelson) blames the property developers for the desecration of the cemetery and sees himself and his family as innocent victims of the ghosts, the Freelings were the first family to move into the suburb and Steven Freeling is himself a realtor selling houses on the estate. It is implied that they are appropriate targets for retribution because they are furthering the original crime and benefiting from it. Rather than punishing the property developers or ejecting the poltergeist from their house, then, it is the Freelings who are ejected from suburbia. The narrative refuses to allow them to remain and further benefit from the appropriation of the land. Because its lead characters are adults, *Poltergeist* can be more directly satirical about the protagonist's complicity with these corporate forces than films with child protagonists.

However, by ejecting the Freelings, *Poltergeist* also simultaneously moderates its criticism of suburbia and its residents. If the whole suburb is built over a cemetery, it would require the entire destruction of suburbia for the property developers to be punished. However, only the Freeling house is haunted and the defeat of the poltergeist is synchronised with the total destruction of their home only, not the destruction of the entire suburb. The Freelings are scapegoats for the crimes actually performed by the property developers. With their ejection, the property developers and the rest of the suburban residents (including, implicitly, the suburban audience) are absolved of their complicity in this appropriation.

This issue of property development continues within the first Amblin cycle of suburban fantastic films. Property developers are shown to be a disruptive force within suburbia and the pre-teen protagonists work to thwart their ambitions without destroying them completely. For example, in *Gremlins*, the gremlins' anarchic destruction of the town correlates with the activity of a local rich lady Mrs Deagle (Polly Holliday) who has bought many properties in the town and is trying to buy up Dorry's Tavern, the local pub where Kate (Phoebe Cates) works and where 'everyone's dad proposed to everyone's mom'. Mrs Deagle lacks community spirit, seeing everyone as 'deadbeats', and is even cruel to Billy's dog, yet justice is served on behalf of Billy, Kate and the audience when the gremlins invade her mansion home and kill her. At the end, a television announcer mentions that through her death the rest of the town has been saved from her plan to build a chemical plant. *Gremlins* offers a wish-fulfilling resolution to the problem of Mrs Deagle, but the forces that she represents are not so easily dealt with. And Dorry's Tavern has still been destroyed in the process.

In *The Goonies*, the family homes of the pre-teen protagonists face foreclosure so that property developers can build a new country club. These property developers appear directly only near the start and at the end of the film; for the remainder, they are symbolically represented by a family of local thieves. Prompted by Mikey's (Sean Astin) discovery of a treasure map and newspaper clipping for the local area, the characters go on a fantastical voyage to recover the lost treasure of the pirate One-Eyed Willy, pursued by the thieves. Ultimately, they defeat the thieves and also obtain the treasure to miraculously save the 'goon docks' from developers. This offers a similarly wish-fulfilling ending as *Gremlins*, but the protagonists' 'solution' to the problem of the developers is actually quite similar to the developer's own crime. The children defeat the developers by appropriating wealth, just as the developers themselves are attempting to do by forcing the parents to sell up their homes. But since they are children, *The Goonies* downplays this appropriation. The pirate treasure has been originally stolen and the children are justified in claiming it for themselves through the primitive 'law' of finders keepers' and as a reward for their bravery, cleverness and resourcefulness. This is enough to justify their claim in the eyes of the audience and displace all the sense of wrongdoing onto the thieves and the bland property developers.

The *Back to the Future* trilogy offers a sweeping view of small town development by tracing the history of Hill Valley from the beginnings of its settlement as a Wild West frontier town in 1885, to an established suburban development with surrounding farming land in 1955, to a fully developed suburban community in the original 1985, to an *alternate* 1985 where wealth and greed have led to the construction of a casino and hotel complex in the centre, and finally to a technological utopian town centre and hi-tech suburbia in a future 2015. Marty and Doc's misadventures through time continually intersect with issues of wealth and power that are shaping the development of the land for better or worse, and part of their task is to correct the timeline so that the best arrangement of wealth, power and land is made for Marty and his family.

Not only does *Back to the Future*'s historical vision of California reveal in microcosm the effects of multinational capital on small town and suburban development, but it also reveals the importance of the Californian suburb in the construction of the suburban fantastic. *Poltergeist, E.T.* and *Back to the Future* arguably made the Californian suburb and its sensibility the exemplary idealised form of the suburb within representation. The location of Hollywood within the suburbs of L.A. County links the Californian suburb to the allure of the American Dream, embodied by the Hollywood film industry. Although suburban fantastic films are set in many different styles of small town and suburb, and such representations diverge visually from the suburbs that many in the audience actually live in, the modern Californian suburb offers an idealisation of suburbia that undermines any criticisms made about it. The representation of suburbia has become, in Ryan Poll's words 'a global form that naturalizes and normalizes both Americanization and capitalism, and it interpellates subjects — regardless of race and ethnicity — as First World consumers' (Poll 2012: 138).

After the first Amblin cycle, the motif of property development continues in various forms in films like *The Gate, *batteries not included*, and twenty-first century suburban fantastic films such as *Monster House* and *Earth to Echo* (Dave Green, 2014). It reveals the otherwise invisible productive force that is literally responsible for the development of the suburban world that the characters occupy. Although suburbia can appear 'natural', it is a constructed space produced by particular historical forces. David Harvey describes a process by which the surplus value created by capitalism became invested in the construction of space that will perpetuate the production of surplus value (Harvey 1991: 184–5), and characterises this space as contemporary suburbia. As the end-product of a certain financial circulation, then, suburbia is a kind of factory, in which individual consumers are produced. Their own rebellious instincts will be tamed, controlled or expelled, in order to create 'heroes' who will replicate the system of capital accumulation. This consumer-hero is not just the protagonist; it is also the spectator, who will either continue to consume such representations, or will grow up into a Hollywood filmmaker and end up reproducing the sf, horror, fantasy and action tropes that they absorbed in their childhood, tropes destined to be consumed in turn by a future suburban audience. Through the movement of this system, capital accumulation and the creation of surplus value are ensured.

Such large historical forces do not just affect suburban fantastic movies and their audiences. They also affect the production processes of both Hollywood studios and suburban developers. Suburbia was constructed along a prefabricated, factory-line mode of production – the Fordist factory production line (Rowley 2015: 57) – much as Hollywood of the 1950s had been defined by forms of factory line production (Bordwell, Staiger and Thompson 2005: 92–5). However, by the 1980s, as Noel Brown notes, Hollywood was changing under the pressure of international capital:

> The structural centrality of family entertainment is closely linked with the processes of multimedia conglomeration that took place in Hollywood in the 1980s and 1990s, when all of the major Hollywood studios, except Disney, were either acquired by larger multinational corporations or merged with other media companies. (Brown 2017: 54)

Suburban fantastic cinema implicitly reflects this process in its representation of contemporary suburbia. By using suburban iconography and a narrative involving the intrusion of fantastic productive forces into suburbia, suburban fantastic films can be read as commenting upon the productive forces shaping Hollywood and society in general. This helps explain why suburbia, and Californian suburbia in particular, is privileged as the location of suburban fantastic films, even though many suburban fantastic films are set in different urban, small town and rural spaces.

## Conclusion

As we have seen, the productive force of multinational capital stands behind the governmental, military, scientific and corporate institutions that are implicated in the intrusion of the element of the fantastic into suburbia. The protagonists are confronted by a world in which the land that the suburb was built on was sacred ground and the construction of the suburb was an act of desecration, an appropriation by business interests (*Poltergeist, The Gate, Monster House*) in order to provide a safe space with the purpose of creating brave white, middle-class males, both producers and consumers, who will support and further the prosperity of the suburb (*Back to the Future, The Goonies*), its local businesses (*Jumanji*), its military values (*Cloak and Dagger, Matinee*) and global corporations (*Small Soldiers*), and contribute to the ever-increasing commercialisation of everyday life. It is the productive force of multinational capital which is the genuinely strange or weird fantastic element that is intruding into the protagonists' everyday lives. And many different kinds of fantastic element – from magical commodities to the bucolic 'natural' space of suburbia itself – offer mystified or distorted reflections of these forces of production. The agents of these forces can either be defeated or co-opted by the protagonist, but either way the forces they represent persist.

Despite the box-office success of suburban fantastic films and the influence of suburban fantastic semantics and syntax within other genres, suburban fantastic films have never since achieved the same cultural prominence as they had in the five years after *E.T.* The suburban fantastic sub-genre was diluted through being blended with other genres, in particular the resurgent family film of the 1990s. By the late 1990s, the audience base for such family films was eroding as a generation of middle-class children began to head to university. Indeed, the combined box-office failure of two of the best suburban fantastic movies, Amblin's *Small Soldiers* in 1998 and Disney's *The Iron Giant* in 1999, was probably the primary reason that the early 2000s saw a decline in production of suburban fantastic cinema.

Other forces were also at work, however. Suburban fantastic films emerged in the Reagan years and are part of a general tendency in the period to resituate the white patriarchal middle-class family at the centre of American self-identity (See Wood, 2003). Films related to the suburban fantastic such as *Wargames, Red Dawn, Cloak and Dagger, Back to the Future, The Manhattan Project, Russkies, Matinee, Small Soldiers* and *The Iron Giant* are also hyper-conscious of Cold War anxieties, frequently deploying images of 'duck and cover' and atomic bomb detonations. By the early 2000s, these cultural preoccupations were fading; fear of terrorism became the dominant political anxiety and this removed the historical background that could anchor further suburban fantastic films.

However, none of these changes were enough to kill the sub-genre entirely. After twenty years, suburban fantastic had become a firm part of Hollywood's pool of generic possibilities. The post-2000 period saw a turn to new kinds of teen-focused weird suburbia (*Donnie Darko* (Richard Kelly, 2001), *The Butterfly Effect* (Eric Bress and J. Mackye Gruber, 2004)), and the continued inclusion of suburban fantastic material within teen narratives (the *Twilight* franchise (2008–12)) and blockbuster cinema (*Harry Potter and the Philosopher's Stone* (Chris Columbus, 2001), *Transformers* (Michael Bay, 2007), *Iron Man 3* (Shane Black, 2013)). Indeed, the 2000s saw a general resurgence of child-focused fantasy cinema based on pre-established literary properties mainly from before the advent of the suburban fantastic in the 1980s (*The Chronicles of Narnia: The Lion, the Witch and the Wardrobe* (Andrew Adamson, 2005), *Charlie and the Chocolate Factory* (Tim Burton, 2005), *Eragon* (Stefan Fangmeier, 2006), *Bridge to Terabithia* (Gabor Csupo, 2007), *The Golden Compass* (Chris Weitz, 2007), *The Dark is Rising* (David L. Cunningham, 2007)). The prominence of these children's fantasies changed the surrounding generic context of contemporary suburban fantastic cinema.

Nevertheless, films that adhered to the traditional semantic and syntactic mixture of the suburban fantastic, such as *Zathura: A Space Adventure, Monster House, Frankenweenie, The Hole* and *Goosebumps* (Rob Letterman, 2015), continued to be produced. They exhibit fidelity to the sub-genre, but they also alter a critical aspect of suburban fantastic narratives: they loosen the connection between the protagonists and the element of the fantastic, often reducing the protagonist's personal melodrama to an issue of overcoming anger or fear. For example, *Zathura: A Space Adventure*, a quasi-sequel to *Jumanji*, focuses on the personal tensions between two brothers (Josh Hutcherson, Jonah Bobo) who blame each other for their parents separating and compete for the attention and approval of their father. They find a 1950s-style space board game in the basement and when they play it, the scenarios become real and their house is suddenly floating in the orbit of Saturn, being bombarded by meteorites, and attacked by alien pirates the Zorgons. But the relationship between the brothers' melodrama and the fantastic is unclear. Neither of them is notably a fan of sf or board games, nor do the scenarios they're presented with particularly correlate to their interpersonal conflict. There is not even a symbolic explanation about why the board game is magical. Simply, it provides an opportunity to stage and resolve their conflict in a heightened form. And because we never see beyond the house into the rest of the suburban street or see people outside the family members, the story is detached from a larger political or historical context.

The Dan Harmon-scripted CGI-animation *Monster House* from Amblin exhibits similar problems. It is a suburban fantastic film that draws on the haunted house horror sub-genre. The main 12-year-old characters DJ (Mitchel Musso) and Charles 'Chowder' (Sam Lerner) think they are too old for trick or treating at Halloween, are experiencing the onset of puberty, and are competing for the affections of Jenny (Spencer Locke). At the same time, they are threatened by a neighbouring house, once owned by a gluttonous woman who was persecuted by trick or treaters and fell into the foundations and died. Her spirit possessed the house and now swallows up children's toys and tries to eat people as well.

Unfortunately, the haunted house has only a loose relation to the personal dramas of the boys. DJ and Chowder don't suffer from excessive appetites or a sense of greed that would correlate with the ghost possessing the house. Nor is there any 'television watching' scene or sense that DJ and Chowder are fans of horror movies, that might explain why their personal issues are manifested through a haunted house. *Monster House* gestures to the multinational productive forces shaping the boys' childhood in that, a few streets away, a lake has been drained to make way for luxury towers; the building site, JCB and crane become features of the final battle against the house. But this property development does not have any obvious effect on the children's quality of life. Instead, at the end, by releasing her spirit, DJ and Chowder are simply reconciled to the idea of remaining children a bit longer by still trick or treating for Halloween and a stable hierarchy has emerged in their competition for Jenny (DJ is preferred but Chowder is also 'liked'). The adventure leaves the characters largely unchanged. The personal problems that have been symbolically resolved are entirely minor.

Both *Zathura* and *Monster House* testify to the weakened link between the element of the fantastic and the interiority of the main protagonist. The looser arrangement is indicated by the fact that the television watching scene that anchors the consciousness of the main protagonist to images from old science fiction and horror movies is missing from both films. They also neglect the political and social elements of the genre. *Zathura*

DJ (Mitchel Musso) and Chowder (Sam Lerner) try to save Jenny (Spencer Locke) in *Monster House* (2006).

was another box-office disappointment, but Amblin's *Monster House* was successful and both have experienced long lives on DVD. They satisfied a continuing desire for suburban fantastic films at the time, but they didn't go as far as to reconceive the sub-genre.

Veterans of the sub-genre such as Tim Burton and Joe Dante also produced further iterations in this period, but they similarly exhibited a looser connection between the personal dilemmas of the protagonist and the element of the fantastic. In Burton's stopmotion/CGI film *Frankenweenie*, Victor Frankenstein (Charlie Tahan), an intelligent boy in a 50s-style suburbia, avoids other members of his class and isolates himself in his interest in science and his friendship with his dog. When his dog dies, Victor reanimates him in the manner of his literary namesake. His classmates find out about this and they try similar experiments which go awry, creating monsters; but ultimately, Victor manages to bring events under control, and even magically gets his dog back at the end, having learnt not to neglect human friendships. Although this also follows the suburban fantastic model, Victor's attempt to resurrect his dead dog, which brings a group of misfits together, is a strange solution to his social isolation. The moral crime of reanimating the dead is largely unaddressed and any larger melodramatic conflict with his father or friends or even himself is prevented by the persistent pastiche of Universal's 1931 *Frankenstein* and other monster movies. Victor's interest in science and reanimation comes from the fact that he 'is' Victor Frankenstein, rather than the fact that he has watched a lot of Universal horror films. Similarly, in Joe Dante's *The Hole*, the fantastic and melodrama are imperfectly aligned. Two brothers Dane (Chris Massoglia) and Lucas (Nathan Gamble) who have moved to a new town, discover a magical hole under their house that manifests their fears. Although the boys and their neighbour Julie (Haley Bennett) individually face their fears and close the hole at the end, the hole itself is never given any clear provenance. Both *Frankenweenie* and *The Hole* include scenes of television watching – *Frankenweenie* shows *Dracula* (Terence Fisher, UK, 1958) and *The Hole* shows *Gorgo* (Eugene Lourie, UK/USA/Ireland, 1961) – but the choice of film is only tangentially connected to the specific element of the fantastic that appears in each film.

*Goosebumps*, an adaptation of the long-running popular pre-teen novel series *Goosebumps* by R.L. Stine, has been the most successful mainstream suburban fantastic film in recent years, but even here the monsters that terrorise the town are not linked to the imagination of Zach (Dylan Minnette), the main teen character, who has little obvious interest in monsters and horror. Instead they are linked to the imagination of the adult character Mr Stine (Jack Black). Stine admits he was lonely as a boy and angry at the world so he imagined these creatures into existence. Practically they are manifested by typing on a supernatural typewriter, but no explanation is given for this typewriter. Zach accidentally releases the monsters from the manuscripts, but it is Stine who resolves the crisis by writing another story featuring all of the monsters which allows him to trap them back into one book. Through this adventure, Stine has confronted his own fears of other people and he ends reintegrated into the community, teaching in the school and dating Zach's aunt. The larger thematic meaning of the intrusion of the fantastic appears to come as a warning against anger, loneliness and the dangers of imagination. But the resolution of Zach's problems – reconnecting with his mother, gaining a real love-interest, and implicitly coming to terms with his grief at his absent father – happens separately to the intrusion of the fantastic. In fact, the intrusion of the fantastic largely functions to advertise many of the favourite monsters and villains of the *Goosebumps* book series, in a further expression of the commercial aspects of the suburban fantastic.

Suburban fantastic films since 2000, then, suffer from similar problems: a looser relationship between the main characters and the fantastic; an over-emphasis on resolving formulaically personal melodramas of the characters that are themselves formulaic; and a commitment to older styles of the fantastic which are unconnected to the contemporary anxieties of pre-teens and teenagers. Here the suburban fantastic cinema functions as safe family films with tepid character dynamics and mildly illogical scenarios. This is manifest most fully in a run of CGI animated suburban fantastic films. *Monster House* is a fairly orthodox entry, but we might also include other family fantasy films set in suburbia and featuring pre-teens such as *Meet the Robinsons* (Steve Anderson 2007), *Aliens in the Attic* (John Schultz, 2009), *Monsters Vs Aliens* (Conrad Vernon and Rob Letterman, 2009), *Mars Needs Moms* (Simon Wells, 2011), *Home* (Tim Johnson, 2015) and *Big Hero 6* (Don Hall and Chris Williams, 2016).

*A Suburban Fantastic Revival: Super 8, Stranger Things, IT*

The first indication of a revival of interest in the suburban fantastic was a trend of remaking films such as *Race to Witch Mountain* (Andy Flickman, 2009), *A Nightmare on Elm Street* (Samuel Bayer, 2010), *Fright Night* (Craig Gillespie, 2011) and *Poltergeist* (Gil Kenan, 2015). This echoes the way that suburban fantastic cinema of the early 80s was accompanied by a series of remakes of 50s sf and horror classics that were themselves inspirations for the suburban fantastic – *Invasion of the Body Snatchers* (Philip Kaufman, 1978), *The Thing* (John Carpenter, 1982), *The Twilight Zone: The Movie*, *The Fly* (David Cronenberg, 1986), *Invaders from Mars* and *The Blob* (Chuck Russell, 1988). The appearance of such remakes indicates the turning of a generational cycle and the possibility of new generic iterations emerging.

Indeed, the changing social, political, technological and demographic landscape of America in the 2010s has created the ground for the revival of the suburban fantastic in a new form, and so a new generation of writers and directors have emerged, interested in producing new suburban fantastic films. Perhaps inevitably, Steven Spielberg has played a role in this. In the 2000s, Spielberg continued to explore the interaction of suburban culture and fantasy narratives in *AI: Artificial Intelligence* (2001), *War of the Worlds* (2005), *The BFG* (2016) and *Ready Player One* (2018), without returning to the suburban fantastic itself. However, in 2011, Spielberg and Amblin produced *Super 8* (J.J. Abrams, 2011), a story about a group of pre-teens in 1979 who witness a train accident that releases an alien being into their suburban town. This film follows the suburban fantastic narrative closely;

ultimately the kids help the alien to escape from the government forces hunting it and simultaneously resolve their own personal melodramas.

What is most striking about *Super 8* though is the way it evokes, through image, music and tone, the feel of previous suburban fantastic films. Shots of boys on bikes, pre-teen bedrooms cluttered with film and science posters, low-lit family scenes with TV screens in the background, the intrusion of the military, and the destruction of suburbia all make its generic ancestry clear. This attempt to replicate previous suburban fantastic films on the level of an aesthetic is a new development in the history of the suburban fantastic. There has always been a degree of reflexivity even in the early Amblin suburban fantastic films – *E.T.* is itself cited in various ways in *Gremlins*, *Back to the Future*, *Explorers*, *Flight of the Navigator* and *The Monster Squad* – but there it was at the level of allusion. *Making Contact* and *Mac & Me* were at times direct imitations, rip-offs even, of *E.T.* But *Super 8* takes allusion and imitation a step further by consciously reflecting the iconography of the Amblin films of the 1980s. The film reuses conventions from classic suburban fantastic films in order to affirm the conventions and the affects that the viewer has already experienced.

*Super 8* was a critical and box-office success and it anticipates others films and television shows that consciously attempt to reproduce the aesthetic of these films. *Stranger Things* (TV, 2016–) is a highly successful Netflix television show, which is even more self-conscious about its tonal and stylistic imitation of suburban fantastic cinema. The focus is placed on three friends, Mike (Finn Wolfhard), Dustin (Gaten Matarazzo) and Lucas

Suburbia under attack in *Super 8* (2011).

(Caleb McLaughlin), and their fourth friend Will (Noah Schnapp) who has gone missing in a parallel universe called the Upside Down. Their quest to save their friend provides the basis of a meta-referential suburban fantastic story. The four friends evoke the dynamic of the kids in *The Goonies*, *Stand by Me* or *Russkies*; their protection of a strange girl called Eleven (Millie Bobby Brown) hunted by the government, harkens to *E.T.: The Extra-Terrestrial*; Will's entrapment in the walls of the house imitate *Poltergeist*; and Joyce's (Winona Ryder) quest to save her son Will recalls the obsessive Roy Neary in *Close Encounters*.

In fact, the allusions to previous suburban films or 80s films in general work on multiple levels. The casting of Winona Ryder, star of *Beetlejuice* and *Edward Scissorhands* helps link the story back to the suburban-set fantasy stories of the 1980s and 90s. The font of the title in the show's credits evokes the original paperbacks of Stephen King, a key reference for the show's small-town mysteries. The synthesiser music recalls John Carpenter's film scores. And an episode title 'The Weirdo on Maple Street' alludes to a *Twilight Zone* episode 'The Monsters Are Due on Maple Street' (TV, 1960), a proto-suburban fantastic story. This indicates the extent to which its creators, the Duffer Brothers, are adhering to the conventions of suburban fantastic cinema, while also going beyond classic suburban fantastic films of the 1980s and drawing on affiliated works as well.

Indeed, *Stranger Things* updates the fantastic for the contemporary audience. Rather than drawing on sf and monster tropes from 1950s cinema, *Stranger Things* offers versions of popular monster and sf films of the 1980s. The creature of the Upside Down evokes the xenomorph of the *Alien* franchise (1979–) while the zone of the Upside Down reflects the Other Side of the *Poltergeist* series. By drawing on blockbuster sf and horror films of the 1980s (particular those of John Carpenter, David Cronenberg and the film adaptations of the writings of Stephen King) *Stranger Things* refreshes its suburban fantastic narrative and displays an understanding of the genre's relationship to the violent action, sf and horror films of the 1980s.

In fact, by including storylines focused on teenagers, a terrorised mother and a local sheriff, *Stranger Things* demonstrates practically the interrelationship of suburban fantastic cinema with John Hughes-style teen romance, supernatural teen horror, and cop mysteries set in weird small towns. The inclusion of these other genres allows *Stranger Things'* female characters to come to the fore rather than being sidelined. And by combining the suburban fantastic model with genres that were consolidated in the 1980s, *Stranger Things* functions something like a comprehensive overview of the suburban fantastic and indicates its central position with the generic field of the 1980s.

Finally, *IT* also exhibits the tonal and stylistic imitation of suburban fantastic movies. Stephen King's 1985 novel appeared contemporaneously with the first cycle of Amblin-produced suburban fantastic cinema and is the most popular and comprehensive literary version of the suburban fantastic. However, the 2017 film adaptation excludes the adult part of the narrative and updates it from 1957 to 1988–89, a period between the novel's original publication and its TV adaptation in 1990. These changes bring *IT*'s narrative about a group of children who are being terrorised by a supernatural child-killer and who band together to defeat it, closer to typical suburban fantastic narratives. The trope of 'overcoming fear', common to the suburban fantastic (cf. *A Nightmare on Elm Street, Cocoon, The Hole* amongst many others) is used: Pennywise the clown, the form 'it' most commonly assumes, is linked to all of the children through their fears and so confronting Pennywise involves each of the protagonists confronting what scares them the most. The story also implies that Pennywise is an emanation of adulthood that is threatening to the kids, a general expression of what grown-up society does to kids in raising them. This is emphasised by the uniformly negative representations of the kids' parents who are at best emotionally distant and at worst abusive. In this, *IT* follows the implication of films like *Stand by Me* and *The Sandlot* that it is the protagonist's ambiguous feelings about adulthood that is generally responsible for the presence of the fantastic.

All of these narrative choices consciously position *IT* within the suburban fantastic model in a way that the choices of the television adaptation of 1990 do not. Furthermore, the film supports this narrative by deploying a complex set of stylistic indicators familiar to classic suburban fantastic films. We continually see the group of friends riding on their bikes through the local streets. Bill (Jaeden Lieberher) has posters of *Gremlins* and *Beetlejuice* on his bedroom walls, and the local cinema hoarding features screenings of *Batman* (Tim Burton, 1989) and *Lethal Weapon 2* (Richard Donner, 1989) prominently displayed. The production design and period detail make it clear that the story is set in the 1980s. But the architecture of the town of Derry, the set design and the details of characters' lives also evoke the 1950s, the original period setting of the novel. In fact, *IT* attempts a curious historical layering: it draws on the iconography of the safe and comfortable 1950s and brings it forward into a representation of the 1980s in order to indicate to an audience of 2017 that the 1980s were just as safe, calm and comfortable as the 1950s. *IT* accepts uncritically the correlation made by 1980s suburban fantastic films between the 80s and the 50s, and does so to once again sell an image of an idyllic and innocent space in culture, which can only be recaptured through consuming images of it. The success of *IT* testifies to the continuing market for such images, and other films such as *Midnight Special* and *Summer of '84* (François Simard, Anouk Whissell, and Yoann-Karl Whissell, 2018), have continued to explore self-consciously the narratives and iconography of suburban fantastic cinema.

*Characteristics of the Reflexive Suburban Fantastic*

The success of these new 'reflexive' suburban fantastic films indicate that the sub-genre is experiencing a cultural prominence that it hasn't had since the early 1980s. Yet these reflexive suburban fantastic films exhibit certain shared traits that distinguish them from previous iterations of the model.

Firstly, reflexive suburban fantastic films are responding to a new generational sensibility. The generation that grew up watching suburban fantastic cinema – dubbed millennials by William Strauss and Neil Howe – has come of age as an adult generation interested in looking back on the culture of their youth. In addition, a generation of new film-makers born in the late 70s–early 80s, such as David Lowery, Jeff Nichols, the Duffer Brothers and Andy Muschietti, are inspired by the suburban fantastic and are incorporating it into their work. However, these directors take a different approach to the suburban fantastic directors of previous decades. Reflexive suburban fantastic films are not addressing the way that suburban childhood is lived today (although see the attempts of *Earth to Echo* to acknowledge contemporary technological change). Nor are they paying cinematic homage to childhood in the 1980s (there are few intelligible references to socio-political events of the time, such as the Challenger disaster or Reagan's 'Star Wars' defence program). Rather, these directors are pastiching the films they liked as kids to an audience that grew up with the originals; that is, they are doing what the makers of suburban fantastic in the 1980s largely didn't do, which was to return to the time period of their youth and make films in the entirely same genre as those they had enjoyed in their youth. In this sense, films like *Super 8* and *Stranger Things* are closer to *Jaws*, Spielberg's version of a 1950s small town monster movie, than they are to *Poltergeist* and *E.T*, which were present-set films defining a new blend of suburban melodrama and the fantastic. Reflexive suburban fantastic films don't pioneer a new blend but revive an old and familiar sub-genre.

Secondly, reflexive suburban fantastic cinema returns to the perspective of lower middle-class suburbia (*Super 8, Midnight Special, Stranger Things, IT*), a world that was represented in the earliest suburban fantastic of *Close Encounters* and *Explorers* but which disappeared in the 90s studio productions for solidly middle-class family audiences. Reflexive suburban fantastic films reconnect with genuine social types and escape from suburban clichés, depicting families experiencing economic and social unease, something which chimes with audiences after the 2007–8 financial crash. This gives reflexive suburban fantastic films a harder edge than conventional family films. The personal melodramas involve trauma and carry psychological weight. The fantastic once again inspires genuine fear and terror in their audience rather than mere thrills. This harder edge appears especially when they emerge as passion projects by indie directors (*Midnight Special*) or receive greater freedom through adult ratings (*IT* was made for an R rating) or supportive studios (Netflix for *Stranger Things*).

Thirdly, reflexive suburban fantastic films take the audience to a place of comfort, safety and security by delivering again the wonder and happiness that they associate with the original suburban fantastic films. Confronted with the instability of the twenty-first century, the millennial generation is returning to its symbolic childhood of the 1980s and retrofitting it as a safe, comfortable space, in which it can psychologically shelter. Rather than locating the invisible productive forces of the present back in the 1950s (and therefore recycling 1950s iconography and cultural references), these new suburban fantastic films locate these forces in the 1980s themselves. The setting of *Super 8* in 1979 places it just on the cusp of the beginning of Amblin's first cycle of suburban fantastic movies. *Stranger Things* is set in 1983, at the height of the first Amblin cycle. And *IT* is set in 1988–89, when the sub-genre began to combine with the family film. Reagan's 1980s, then, have superseded Eisenhower's 1950s as the ideological time-period *par excellence*, as the focus of sentimental nostalgia for a vanished idyllic past. Setting suburban fantastic films thirty years in the past, however, is also part of the sub-genre's tradition. Even though most of the original suburban fantastic films were set in the present (i.e. 1980s and 90s), *Back to the Future*, *Matinee* and *The Iron Giant* return to the 50s and 60s to nostalgically bask in the culture of that time.

Returning to the fact that reflexive suburban fantastic films represent the 1980s through imitations of previous representations, we can see that rather than blending suburban melodrama and pastiches of 50s horror and sf, reflexive suburban fantastic cinema pastiches the suburban fantastic itself. And a show like *Stranger Things* combines this pastiche with imagery of the fantastic sourced from violent action, fantasy and horror films of the 1980s. This is a development with interesting consequences.

By pastiching the suburban fantastic within itself, reflexive suburban fantastic films promote the emergence of the suburban fantastic itself as a definable sub-genre. As Richard Dyer asserts, pastiche can be an intervention in defining genre: 'it is a pastiche that contributes to bringing the genre more firmly into existence by indicating that it already exists' (Dyer 2007: 118). So today, the modern pastiches of suburban fantastic cinema are revealing the contours of the sub-genre all the more clearly and establishing it as a significant sub-genre.

Like the pastiches of 50s sf and horror films in the original suburban fantastic of the 1980s and 90s, the pastiches in reflexive suburban fantastic films are a way of alerting the viewer to what Dyer calls the 'historicity of our feelings' (Dyer 2007: 130). The affects delivered by reflexive suburban fantastic films have their roots in the 1940s, 1950s and 1980s. 1940s small-town family films linked small-town iconography with a sense of comfort and security. Sf and horror films of the 1950s consolidated a new form of fear and terror that became familiar and homely when repeated in films of the 1980s. And suburban fantastic films of the 1980s complemented this with a new sense of wonder appropriate to a new hyper-commercialised capitalism. Now the reflexive suburban fantastic of the 2010s consciously deploys nostalgia to intensify the experience of consuming the film. Nostalgia has been a part of suburban fantastic cinema from the beginning, but suburban fantastic films have progressively reoriented the feeling of nostalgia from the 1950s (*Back to the Future*), to the 60s (*Jumanji*) and 70s (*Super 8*). Now the reflexive suburban fantastic of the 2010s redirects its nostalgia back towards the 1980s, the production period of the original cycle of Amblin films, to create what Fredric Jameson calls 'nostalgia films,' films where 'the image – the surface sheen of a period fashion reality – is consumed, having been transformed into a visual commodity' (Jameson 2011: 179). Childhood is the object of nostalgia *par excellence* and has motivated the suburban fantastic throughout its history, but in reflexive suburban fantastic cinema, the spectator consumes *as a commodity* their childhood-movie nostalgia, a nostalgia that intensifies the consumption to an even greater degree.

By pastiching suburban fantastic films, then, reflexive suburban fantastic films betray a conservative desire to produced consolidated, 'classical' versions, rather than new risky variants. By contrast, suburban fantastic films of the 1990s and even non-reflexive suburban fantastic like *Frankenweenie* and *Goosebumps* continue innovating with the sub-genre, making unlikely genre combinations as part of the general field of possibilities in Hollywood family entertainment. However, the images and narratives of reflexive suburban fantastic films are saturated with echoes of previously consumed suburban fantastic works. Their narratives and *mise-en-scène* are hyper-commodified. There are few genuine criticisms of government, military or corporate forces that are not already conventional tropes. And there is a continuing focus on the white, middle-class, male pre-teen, or the pre-dominantly male friendship group, as the central figure whose melodramas matter in contemporary society.

*Media, Multinational Capital, Masculinity*

These new reflexive suburban fantastic films of the 2010s, then, are an ambiguous development. As some of their traits indicate, they do not manage to completely avoid the problem that has affected the conventionalized studio-produced suburban fantastic stories of the 2000s and 2010s; that is, the looser relation between the pre-teen protagonist and the element of the fantastic. Indeed, this looser relation remains the defining trait of contemporary suburban fantastic production and affects the representation of the invisible productive forces (media, multinational capital and masculinity) that are most often condensed in the element of the fantastic.

*Media*

Recent suburban fantastic films respond to the changed technological situation of the present. The suburban fantastic films of the 1980s were premised on the disruptive effect that television had within the domestic environment. Yet in the thirty years since suburban fantastic cinema began, domestic media technology has been transformed. Land lines, VHS recorders, camcorders and the PC have been replaced by wireless internet, smartphones, laptops, video games and DVDs. Reflexive suburban fantastic films tend to be set in the 1980s and so easily avoid the new technology, although *Super 8* shows the kids making their own film on super 8 cameras, an early precursor to contemporary smartphone filming technology of the present. Instead, it is present-set suburban fantastic films such as *Poltergeist* and *Earth to Echo* that are best positioned to register the changed technological environment. The remake of *Poltergeist* begins with images from a video game played on a tablet suggesting that it is the modern violent excesses of new technology that lie behind the appearance of the poltergeist. The Bowen family's smart phones, wireless internet, laptops, drones and GPS technology are visually implicated in the presence of the poltergeist, alongside the older technology of the electrical power lines that, we're told, cause tumours, and, apparently, poltergeists. Likewise, *Earth to Echo* attempts with some success to make mobile phone and internet technology the basis of its story about a group of kids finding a robot alien and helping him recover his spacecraft. The robot alien disrupting the lives of Alex (Teo Halm), Tuck (Brian Bradley), Munch (Reese Hartwig) and Emma (Ella Wahlestedt) first appears through a signal interrupting their mobile phones, as if it is now smart mobile phones and internet culture generally that is disrupting their lives. *Earth to Echo* also adopts the conceit similar to found-footage horror films: that it is filmed by one of the characters as it happens and edited together after the fact. This goes some way to formally innovating away from the traditional aesthetics of suburban fantastic cinema.

Arguably, this new technological dispensation should have influenced the elements of the fantastic that appear within these present-set suburban fantastic films as well, but instead, they tend to draw on the sf, horror and fantasy of 1980s blockbusters or the kinds of fantastic that appear in 1980s suburban fantastic films. For example, *Earth to Echo* relies heavily on an *E.T.* style encounter, which sits oddly with the use of modern technology, and the ghost in the *Poltergeist* remake is largely unchanged from the original. Although these films acknowledge the changed technological situation, they struggle to align this with the element of the fantastic.

In reflexive suburban fantastic films, the overwhelming influence of movies on the characters is stressed, yet movies are also diffused in a general media environment that loosens the connection between the pre-teen protagonists and media. In *Super 8,* the main protagonists are huge movie fans making their own zombie-noir film and this acknowledges that the invisible productive force lying behind their lives is cinema itself. However, the escaped alien and military take-over of their town are not related directly to the zombie-noir film they are making. In fact, the characters completely fail to connect what is happening in their town to the sf and horror movies they love. *Super 8* therefore sits uneasily with its generic antecedents, as if acknowledging them too closely might tip *Super 8* into parody rather than homage. *Stranger Things* solves this problem by showing the characters being enthusiastic about sf horror films of the 1980s and having the Demi-gorgon monster echo the monsters of such films. Through this, *Stranger Things* creates a stronger connection between the protagonists' televisual viewing and the element of the fantastic, but it still avoids showing clips of suburban fantastic films and doesn't comment directly on the similarity of its plot to classic suburban fantastic films.

Reflexive suburban fantastic films, then, exhibit a contradictory attitude towards media. On the one hand, movies saturate the characters' perceptions of everyday life. On the other hand, this saturation is less significant when the characters' environment is already saturated by the media culture of the 1980s. This is manifested in the diminished presence of the television watching scene in 80s-set narratives. Television tends to display the wider cultural ephemera (news, adverts, gameshows) of the historical moment rather than specific movies that relate to the element of the fantastic. Instead generic affiliations to sf and horror movies are mainly conveyed through movie posters. Thus, we find Joe in *Super 8* has posters of *Dawn of the Dead* (George Romero, 1978) and *Halloween*. In *Stranger Things*, the main characters have posters of *The Thing* and *The Evil Dead* (Sam Raimi, 1981) and allude to getting tickets to see the 1982 *Poltergeist*. And in *IT*, Bill has posters of *Gremlins* and *Beetlejuice* hanging in his bedroom. However, elements of the fantastic do not clearly emerge out of the repertoire of tropes indicated by these posters. In *IT*, there is no sense that Bill or any of the kids are horror or sf fans, despite the posters, nor does Pennywise evoke any of the images they have seen in films. These posters indicate the characters' viewing habits and the media culture that they inhabit. But the lack of a specific movie linking to the element of the fantastic loosens the connection between the element of the fantastic and media.

*Multinational Capital*

The representation of multinational capital which underlies the appearance of the fantastic is also affected by the looser relation between the protagonist and the element of the fantastic. In general, recent suburban fantastic films are curiously unanchored from the historical and political realities of the 1980s. *Super 8* resurrects a version of the pop culture trope of Area 51, which derives from a weather-balloon accident in 1947. *Stranger Things* draws on real-life conspiracy histories involving CIA/ MKUltra experiments into mind-control, telekinesis and other paranormal powers, but these have also been staples of conspiracy thrillers since *The X-Files* (TV, 1993–2018). *Earth to Echo* reveals that the developers of the new freeway are aligned with the government agents investigating the alien. The iconography of federal agents, military soldiers and scientists is recycled without being connected with the genuine socio-political forces of the periods.

Indeed, recent suburban fantastic films appear to be rather comfortable with aspects of contemporary American society (property development, military values, government and business) that were targets of criticism in previous suburban fantastic films. For example, both *Super 8* and *Stranger Things* notably turn the local sheriff into a main protagonist rather than a supplementary menacing character. In the remake of *Poltergeist*, the Bowen family are experiencing constrained economics after the financial crash of 2007–8 and move into a house which is cheaper because of property foreclosures, but this fails to lead to any notable criticism of property developers. Similarly, it is difficult to imagine *Stranger Things* making an attack on the culture of the 1980s in the way that *Small Soldiers* attacks product placement and global corporations selling violent kids' toys. By avoiding critical comments on socio-political realities, contemporary suburban fantastic films arguably appear complicit in the ever-extending reign of commodification and commercialisation in contemporary society.

*Masculinity*

What remains most persistent in contemporary suburban fantastic cinema is the gender melodrama of the protagonists. Indeed, *Stranger Things* and *IT* focus on several pre-teen/teenage boys who face different melodramatic situations and confront elements of the fantastic that take multiple forms. It is still possible to tell narratives of maturation and socialisation involving female characters who can learn positive values of responsibility, trust, courage, etc, and become heroes in their own right. But in the main the protagonists of recent suburban fantastic films are still boys who are called on to become heroes, and they do so in ways that do not merely involve benign maturation, but include being socialised into compromises with patriarchy, through subordinating femininity and lower class bullies. For example, in the climax of *IT*, the pre-dominantly male group of kids defeat Pennywise by overcoming their fear but they also essentially gang up on him and beat him up. Inadvertently, they become the bullies and defeat Pennywise in the name of overcoming their own fear of bullying. This is offered without a leavening satiric edge. Even the one girl of the group Beverly (Sophia Lillis) joins in.

This male-focus has persisted even into films that otherwise attempt to do something different with the suburban fantastic formula. For example, *ParaNorman* (Sam Fell and Chris Butler, 2012) tells the story of Norman, a 11-year old boy who has the ability to see ghosts and is therefore ostracised by many in his town. He is charged with protecting the town against a witch's curse and when he fails, the dead rises from their graves and attack the town. However, it is ultimately revealed that the 'witch' is a young girl who could also see the dead like him, and who was executed unjustly as a witch for her ability. This goes some way to linking the film's presentation of witches to the real history of misogyny that led to women being executed as witches. But the story still focuses on the traditional suburban fantastic melodrama of the birth of Norman's heroism in saving the town. Similarly, *Attack the Block* (Joe Cornish, UK, 2011) is set in a London council estate and involves a group of disadvantaged black teenagers defending themselves and their turf against an alien invasion. While this setting brings many welcome alterations to the conventional melodrama of the suburban fantastic, it maintains the sub-genre's traditional neglect of female characters, in favour of a male friendship group and a masculinised fantastic (the invading aliens are males pursuing the scent of a female alien).

*Super 8* interestingly attempts something different: a narrative about overcoming grief, rather than becoming a hero. Joe's main melodrama concerns the fact that his mother has been killed in an industrial accident caused by Alice's drunkard father Louis (Ron Eldard). This melodrama is technically aligned with the appearance of a traumatised alien in his town; and by rescuing Alice and connecting psychically with the alien, Joe overcomes his grief over his mother's death and forgives Alice's father. However, this new melodramatic model doesn't quite work. The connection between Joe and the alien is never firmly established. The alien is an awkward blend of sensitive, lost soul and threatening monster, and is caught between representing Joe's grief about his mother and his anger towards Louis. Furthermore, while he does reconnect with his father, Joe's journey is not entirely a new compromise with a patriarchal inheritance. *Super 8* unsuccessfully experiments with the melodramatic underpinning of the suburban fantastic, but this serves to highlight the importance of adhering to the melodramatic conventions of the sub-genre.

The continuing importance of the male focus in suburban fantastic cinema is evident in the increased focus on father-son relationships in recent films. Where many older suburban fantastic films kept parents at arm's length, as sources of conflict, recent suburban fantastic films treat male adults sympathetically as adults, not grown-up children, a telling generational shift. At times, they even compete for the focus of the story with pre-teen protagonists (for instance, Deputy Jackson (Kyle Chandler) in *Super 8*, R. L. Stine (Jack Black) in *Goosebumps*, Roy Tomlin (Michael Shannon) in *Midnight Special*). By introducing adult perspectives alongside the child's perspective, recent suburban fantastic films reflect the older adult audience of these films and fantasise an alliance between the generations, in which adult males share the male child's experience of the fantastic. Father–son relations are reinforced in recent suburban fantastic films, rather than giving way to a wider spectrum of relations.

*Conclusion*

The enormous success of *Stranger Things* and *IT* shows that the suburban fantastic has a tenacious persistence and is well established as a blend of semantic and syntactic elements which responds over time to changes in pre-teen experience, suburban culture, technology, the prevailing socio-political-historical situation, and the popularity of other genres. Suburban fantastic cinema expresses the wonder and fear experienced by male pre-teens confronted with the imminence of adulthood and mature friendships and romantic relationships. It positions American suburbia as the most natural, healthy and desirable environment imaginable, but also registers the increasing commodification of that environment. It both reveals the disturbing power of cinema and other media images on pre-teen imaginations, and revels in that power. And it registers the concomitant negative effects of multinational capital, the military-industrial complex, and a patriarchal social order on the world, but often validates pre-teen protagonists who accept these as part of the world.

Suburban fantastic narratives, however, are no longer limited to cinema. The revival in suburban fantastic cinema over the last decade has extended the suburban fantastic into fiction (Grady Hendrix's *My Best Friend's Exorcism* (Quirk Books, 2017), Jason Rekulak's *The Impossible Fortress* (Faber, 2017)), comic books (Brian K. Vaughan and Cliff Chiang's *Paper Girls* (Image Comics, 2016–)), animated shows (*Gravity Falls* (Disney, TV, 2012–16), *Rick and Morty* (Cartoon Network, TV, 2013–), *Trollhunters* (Netflix, 2016–)) podcasting (*Welcome to Night Vale*), illustration and photography (the work of Simon Stålenhag, Gregory Crewdson and Shaun Tan) and music (the cover art and music videos of M83). It is clear that the ideological construct of pre-teens growing up in a small town in which something strange or spooky is happening is in no danger of disappearing any time soon but will continue adapting itself to changing socio-economic conditions of the audience and different media formats. As Stephen Rowley says of 'classical suburban narratives', suburban fantastic films are 'not simply period pieces set at an arbitrary distance in the past: they are cultural origin stories, isolating a particular moment in time that was crucial in creating our current way of life' (Rowley 2015: 206). Further seasons of *Stranger Things* and *Trollhunters*, and sequels to *IT* and *Jumanji: Welcome to the Jungle* (Jake Kasdan, 2017) are in the pipeline. Since the 1980s, children have been socialised into performing the roles of consumers in a modern mediatised environment, and suburban fantastic cinema has both promoted the integration of ever more children into the dominant social codes of the historical moment, while also reflecting on this process. Filmmakers and other artists will continue to create new suburban fantastic stories films as long as this process of socialisation continues in a society dominated by conglomeration, franchises and tie-in merchandise. After all, suburban fantastic cinema is a space in which audiences can relive the exhilarating and un-nerving process by which their imaginations and their identities have been commodified and consumed.

# FILMOGRAPHY

*Selected Suburban Fantastic Movies (in order of release)*

*Close Encounters of the Third Kind*. Dir. Steven Spielberg. Columbia
    Pictures. 1977. Film.
*Halloween*. Dir. John Carpenter. Compass International/Falcon
    Productions/Debra Hill Productions. 1978. Film.
*Poltergeist*. Dir. Tobe Hooper. Metro-Goldwyn-Mayer. 1982. Film.
*E.T.: The Extra-Terrestrial*. Dir. Steven Spielberg. Universal Pictures. 1982.
    Film.
*The Twilight Zone: The Movie*. Dirs. John Landis, Steven Spielberg, Joe
    Dante, George Miller. Warner Bros. Pictures. 1983. Film.
*Los Nuevos Extraterrestres* (*Extra-Terrestrial Visitors*, a.k.a. *Pod People*).
    Dir. Juan Piquer Simon. Almena Films/France 2/France3. 1983. Film.
*Gremlins*. Dir. Joe Dante. Warner Bros. Pictures. 1984. Film.
*The Last Starfighter*. Dir. Nick Castle. Universal Pictures. 1984. Film.
*Cloak and Dagger*. Dir. Richard Franklin. Universal Pictures. 1984. Film.
*Starman*. Dir. John Carpenter. Columbia Pictures. 1984. Film.
*The Goonies*. Dir. Richard Donner. Warner Bros. Pictures. 1985. Film
*Explorers*. Dir. Joe Dante. Paramount Pictures. 1985. Film.
*Weird Science*. Dir. John Hughes. Universal Pictures. 1985. Film.
*D.A.R.Y.L.* Dir. Simon Wincer. Paramount Pictures/Columbia Pictures.
    1985. Film.
*Back to the Future*. Dir. Robert Zemeckis. Universal. 1985. Film.
*My Science Project*. Dir. Jonathan R. Betuel. Touchstone Pictures/Silver
    Screen Partners II. 1985. Film.

*Making Contact* (a.k.a. *Joey*). Dir. Roland Emmerich. New World Pictures. 1985. Film.

*Cocoon.* Dir. Ron Howard. 20th Century Fox. 1985. Film.

*Fright Night.* Dir. Tom Holland. Columbia Pictures. 1985. Film.

*Short Circuit.* Dir. John Badham. Producers Sales Organization/The Turman Foster Company. 1986. Film.

*Flight of the Navigator.* Dir. Randal Kleiser. Buena Vista Distribution. 1986. Film.

*Invaders from Mars.* Dir. Tobe Hooper. Cannon Pictures. 1986. Film.

*Harry and the Hendersons.* Dir. William Dear. Universal Pictures. 1987. Film.

*The Monster Squad.* Dir. Fred Dekker. Tri-Star Pictures. 1987. Film.

*The Lost Boys.* Dir. Joel Schumacher. Warner Bros. Pictures. 1987. Film.

*Russkies.* Dir. Rick Rosenthal. New Century Vista Film Company. 1987. Film.

*SpaceCamp.* Dir. Harry Winer. ABC Motion Pictures. 1987. Film.

*\*batteries not included.* Dir. Matthew Robbins. Amblin Entertainment/ Universal Pictures. 1987. Film.

*The Gate.* Dir. Tibor Takács. New Century Vista Films Company. 1987. Film.

*Stand by Me.* Dir. Rob Reiner. Columbia Pictures. 1987. Film.

*Cocoon: The Return.* Dir. Daniel Petrie. 20th Century Fox. 1988. Film.

*Fright Night Part 2.* Dir. Tommy Lee Wallace. TriStar Pictures. 1988. Film.

*Big.* Dir. Penny Marshall. 20th Century Fox. 1988. Film.

*Watchers.* Dir. Jon Hess. Carolco Pictures/Concorde Pictures/Centaur Films. 1988. Film.

*Mac & Me.* Dir. Stewart Raffill. New Star Entertainment/Vision International. 1988. Film.

*The Wizard.* Dir. Todd Holland. The Finnegan/Pinnchuk Company/Pipeline Productions. 1989. Film.

*Little Monsters.* Dir. Richard Alan Greenberg. United Artists. 1989. Film.

*Honey, I Shrunk the Kids.* Dir. Joe Johnston. Buena Vista Pictures. 1989. Film.

*The 'burbs.* Dir. Joe Dante. Universal Pictures. 1989. Film.

*Home Alone.* Dir. Chris Columbus. 20th Century Fox. 1990. Film.

*Arachnophobia.* Dir. Frank Marshall. Buena Vista Pictures. 1990. Film.

*And You Thought Your Parents Were Weird.* Dir. Tony Cookson. Trimark Pictures. 1991. Film.

*Hocus Pocus*. Dir. Kenny Ortega. Buena Vista Pictures. 1993. Film.

*Matinee*. Dir. Joe Dante. Universal Pictures. 1993. Film.

*The Sandlot*. Dir. David Mickey Evans. 20th Century Fox. 1993. Film.

*The Pagemaster*. Dir. Joe Johnston and Maurice Hunt. 20th Century Fox/ Turner Pictures. 1993. Film.

*Casper*. Dir. Brad Silberling. Universal Pictures. 1995. Film.

*Jumanji*. Dir. Joe Johnston. Tri-Star Pictures. 1995. Film.

*Evolver*. Dir. Mark Rosman. Trimark Pictures. 1995. Film.

*Toy Story*. Dir. John Lasseter. Pixar Animation Studios/Walt Disney Pictures. 1995. Film.

*Star Kid*. Dir. Manny Coto. Trimark Pictures. 1998. Film.

*Small Soldiers*. Dir. Joe Dante. Dreamworks Pictures/Universal Pictures. 1998. Film.

*The Iron Giant*. Dir. Brad Bird. Warner Bros. Pictures. 1999. Film.

*Eight-Legged Freaks*. Dir. Ellory Elkayem. Warner Bros. Pictures. 2002. Film.

*Zathura: A Space Adventure*. Dir. Jon Favreau. Sony Pictures. 2005. Film.

*Monster House*. Dir. Gil Kenan. Columbia Pictures. 2006. Film.

*Disturbia*. Dir. D.J. Caruso. Paramount Pictures. 2007. Film.

*Transformers*. Dir. Michael Bay. Dreamworks Pictures/Paramount Pictures. 2007. Film.

*The Hole*. Dir. Joe Dante. Big Air Studios. 2009. Film.

*Super 8*. Dir. J.J. Abrams. Paramount Pictures. 2011. Film.

*Attack the Block*. Dir. Joe Cornish. StudioCanal Features/Film4/UK Film Council/Big Talk Pictures. 2011. Film.

*Frankenweenie*. Dir. Tim Burton. Walt Disney Studios Motion Pictures. 2012. Film.

*ParaNorman*. Dir. Sam Fell and Chris Butler. Laika. 2012. Film.

*Earth to Echo*. Dir. Dave Green. Relativity Media. 2014. Film.

*Goosebumps*. Dir. Rob Letterman. Columbia Pictures. 2015. Film.

*Midnight Special*. Dir. Jeff Nichols. Warner Bros. Pictures. 2015. Film.

*Pete's Dragon*. Dir. David Lowery. Walt Disney Pictures/Whitaker Entertainment. 2016. Film.

*IT*. Dir. Andy Muschietti. Warner Bros. Pictures. 2017. Film.

*Jumanji: Welcome to the Jungle*. Dir. Jake Kasdan. Sony Pictures Entertainment. 2017. Film.

*Summer of '84*. Dir. François Simard, Anouk Whissell and Yoann-Karl Whissell. Brightlight Pictures/Gunpowder and Sky. 2018. Film.

*Ready Player One*. Dir. Steven Spielberg. Warner Bros. Pictures. 2018. Film.

*The House with a Clock in its Walls*. Dir. Eli Roth. Universal Pictures. 2018. Film.

*Goosebumps 2: Haunted Halloween*. Dir. Ari Sandel. Sony Pictures Releasing. 2018. Film.

*Selected Original TV Series*

*Amazing Stories*. Created by Steven Spielberg. Amblin Entertainment/ Universal Television. 1985–7. TV.

*The Simpsons*. Created by Matt Groening. Fox Television Animation. 1989–present. TV.

*Eerie, Indiana*. Created by José Rivera and Karl Schaefer. Unreality, Inc., Cosgrove/Meurer Productions, Hearst Entertainment. 1991–2. TV.

*Harry and the Hendersons*. Amblin Television/Universal Television. 1991–3. TV.

*Weird Science*. Developed by Tom Spezialy and Alan Cross. St Clare Entertainment/Universal Television. 1994–8. TV.

*Are You Afraid of the Dark?* Created by D. J. MacHale and Ned Kandel. Cinar/Nickelodeon Productions. 1990–6. 1999–2000. TV.

*Goosebumps*. Created by R.L. Stine. Developed by Deborah Forte. Protocol Entertainment/Scholastic Entertainment/Gajdecki Visual Effects. 1995–8 TV.

*Buffy the Vampire Slayer*. Created by Joss Whedon. Mutant Enemy Productions/Sandollar Television/Kuzui Entertainment/20th Century Fox Television. 1997–2003. TV.

*Gravity Falls*. Created by Alex Hirsch. Disney Television Animation. 2013–6. TV.

*Rick and Morty*. Created by Justin Roiland and Dan Harmon. Cartoon Network. 2013–present. TV.

*Stranger Things*. Created by the Duffer Brothers. Netflix. 2016–present. TV.

*Trollhunters*. Created by Guillermo del Toro. Netflix. 2016–present. TV.

# BIBLIOGRAPHY

Allen, Robert C. 'Home Alone Together: Hollywood and the "Family Film"'. Melvyn Stokes and Richard Maltby (eds) *Identifying Hollywood's Audiences: Cultural Identity and the Movies.* London: British Film Institute. 1999: 109–34.

Altman, Rick. *Film/Genre.* London: British Film Institute. 1999.

Avila, Eric. *Popular Culture in the Age of White Flight: Fear and Fantasy in Suburban Los Angeles.* Berkeley and Los Angeles, California: University of California Press. 2006.

Barber, Benjamin R. *Consumed: How Markets Corrupt Children, Infantilize Adults, and Swallow Citizens Whole.* New York and London: W.W. Norton & Company. 2007.

Baxandall, Rosalyn and Elizabeth Ewen, *Picture Windows: How the Suburbs Happened.* New York: Basic Books. 2000.

Bazalgette, Cary and Terry Staples. 'Unshrinking the Kids: Children's Cinema and the Family Film'. Cary Bazalgette and David Buckingham (eds) *In Front of the Children.* London: British Film Institute. 1995: 92–109.

Bellin, Joshua David. *Framing Monsters: Fantasy Film and Social Alienation.* Carbondale: Southern Illinois University Press. 2005.

Bettelheim, Bruno. *The Uses of Enchantment: The Meaning and Importance of Fairy Tales.* London: Penguin. 1976.

Beuka, Robert. *SuburbiaNation: Reading Suburban Landscape in Twentieth Century American Landscape and Film.* New York: Palgrave Macmillan. 2004.

Bordwell, David, Janet Staiger, and Kristin Thompson. *The Classical Hollywood Cinema: Film Style and Mode of Production to 1960.* London: Routledge. 2005.

Broderick, Mick. 'Rebels with a Cause: Children versus the Military Industrial Complex'. Timothy Shary and Alexandra Seibel (eds) *Youth Culture in Global Cinema.* Austin: University of Texas Press. 2007: 37–56.

Brooks, Peter. *The Melodramatic Imagination: Balzac, Henry James, Melodrama and the Mode of Excess.* New Haven: Yale University Press. 1976.

Brown, Noel. *The Hollywood Family Film: A History, from Shirley Temple to Harry Potter.*

London: I.B. Tauris and Co. Ltd. 2012.

Brown, Noel. '"Family" Entertainment and Contemporary Hollywood Cinema'. *Scope: An Online Journal of Film and Television Studies*. No. 25. 2013.

Brown, Noel. 'The "Family" Film, and the Tensions between Popular and Academic Interpretations of Genre'. *Trespassing Journal: An Outline Journal of Trespassing Art, Science and Philosophy*. Issue 2. Winter 2013.

Brown, Noel. *The Children's Film: Genre, Nation, and Narrative*. London/New York: Wallflower Press. 2017.

Brown, Noel, and Bruce Babington (eds). *Family Films in Global Cinema: The World Beyond Disney*. London: I.B. Tauris Co. and Ltd. 2015.

Bruzzi, Stella. *Men's Cinema: Masculinity and Mise-en-scène in Hollywood*. Edinburgh: Edinburgh University Press. 2013.

Butler, David. *Fantasy Cinema: Impossible Worlds on Screen*. London/New York: Wallflower Press. 2009.

Carroll, Noël, 'The Future of Allusion: Hollywood in the Seventies (And Beyond)'. *October*. Vol. 20. Spring. 1982. 51–81.

Coon, David R. *Look Closer: Suburban Narratives and American Values in Film and Television*. New Brunswick, NJ: Rutgers. 2013.

Cross, Gary. *Consumed Nostalgia: Memory in the Age of Fast Capitalism*. New York: Columbia University Press. 2015.

Davis, Blair. *The Battle for the Bs: 1950s Hollywood and the Rebirth of Low-Budget Cinema*. New Brunswick, NJ: Rutgers University Press. 2012.

Dyer, Richard. *Pastiche*. Oxford: Routledge. 2007.

Fowkes, Katherine A. *The Fantasy Film*. Chichester: Wiley-Blackwell. 2010.

Frayling, Christopher. *Mad, Bad and Dangerous?: The Scientist and the Cinema*. London, UK: Reaktion Books. 2006.

Gledhill, Christine. 'The Melodramatic Field: An Investigation', in *Home Is Where the Heart Is: Studies in Melodrama and the Woman's Film*. London: British Film Institute. 1987: 5–39.

Gledhill, Christine and Linda Williams (eds). *Reinventing Film Studies*. London: Hodder Arnold. 2000.

Gordon, Andrew M. *Empire of Dreams: The Science Fiction and Fantasy Films of Steven Spielberg*. Lanham, Maryland: Rowman and Littlefield. 2008.

Harwood, Sarah. *Family Fictions: Representations of the Family in 1980s Hollywood Cinema*. New York: Palgrave Macmillan. 1997.

Harvey, David. *The Condition of Postmodernity: An Enquiry into the Origins of Cultural Change*. Oxford: Blackwell. 1991.

Jackson, Rosemary. *Fantasy: The Literature of Subversion*. London and New York: Routledge. 1981.

Jameson, Fredric. *Marxism and Form: Twentieth-Century Dialectical Theories of Literature*. Princeton, New Jersey: Princeton University Press. 1971.

Jameson, Fredric. *Postmodernism: Or, The Cultural Logic of Late Capitalism*. London: Verso Press. 1991.

Jameson, Fredric. *Signatures of the Visible*. Oxford: Routledge. 2011.

Jeffords, Susan. *Hard Bodies: Hollywood Masculinity in the Reagan Era*. New Brunswick, NJ: Rutgers University Press. 1994.

Kapur, Jyotsna. *Coining for Capital: Movies, Marketing, and the Transformation of Childhood*. New Brunswick, NJ: Rutgers University Press. 2005.

Kendrick, James. *Hollywood Bloodshed: Violence in 1980s American Cinema*. Carbondale: Southern Illinois University Press. 2009.

Kendrick, James. *Darkness in the Bliss-Out: A Reconsideration of the Films of Steven Spielberg*. New York and London: Bloomsbury. 2014.

King, Geoff. *Spectacular Narratives: Hollywood in the Age of the Blockbuster*. London: I.B. Tauris and Co. Ltd. 2000.

Krämer, Peter. 'Would You Take Your Child to See This Film? The Cultural and Social Work of the Family-Adventure Movie'. Steve Neale and Murray Smith (eds) *Contemporary Hollywood Cinema*. London: Routledge. 1998: 294–311.

Krämer, Peter. '"The Best Disney Film Disney Never Made": Children's Films and the Family Audience in American Cinema since the 1960s'. Steve Neale (ed.) *Genre and Contemporary Hollywood*. London: BFI Publishing. 2002: 185–200.

Krämer, Peter. '"It's Aimed at Kids – The Kid in Everyone": George Lucas, *Star Wars* and Children's Entertainment'. Yvonne Tasker (ed.) *Action and Adventure Cinema*. London: Routledge. 2004: 358–70.

Latham, Rob. 'Subterranean Suburbia: Underneath the Smalltown Myth in the Two Versions of *Invaders from Mars*'. *Science-Fiction Studies*. 22.2. July 1995: 198–208.

Latham, Rob. *Consuming Youth: Vampires, Cyborgs, and the Culture of Consumption*. Chicago, IL: University of Chicago Press. 2002.

Lehu, Jean-Marc. *Branded Entertainment: Product Placement & Brand Strategy in the Entertainment Business*. Philadelphia: Kogan Page Ltd. 2008.

Levy, Emanuel. *Small-Town America in Film: The Decline and Fall of Community*. New York: Continuum. 1991.

Lichtenfeld, Eric. *Action Speaks Louder: Violence, Spectacle, and the American Action Movie*. Westport, CT: Praeger Publishers. 2004.

Malcolm, Derek. 'Raiders of the Ugly Duckling'. *The Guardian*. 9 December 1982. 13.

Mallan, Kerry and Clare Bradford (eds). *Contemporary Children's Literature and Film: Engaging with Theory*. London: Palgrave Macmillan. 2011.

MacKinnon, Kenneth. *Hollywood's Small Towns: An Introduction to the American Small-Town Movie*. Metuchen, N.J. & London: Scarecrow Press, 1984.

McBride, Joseph. *Steven Spielberg: A Biography. Third Edition*. London: Faber and Faber. 2012.

Mendlesohn, Farah. *Rhetorics of Fantasy*. Middletown, CT; Wesleyan University Press. 2008.

Mercer, John and Martin Shingler. *Melodrama: Genre, Style, Sensibility*. London/New York: Wallflower Press. 2004.

Messenger Davies, Máire. *Children, Media and Culture*. Berkshire, UK: Open University Press. 2010.

Morris, Nigel. *The Cinema of Steven Spielberg: Empire of Light*. London/New York: Wallflower Press. 2007.

Murphy, Bernice M. *The Suburban Gothic* in American Popular Culture. New York: Palgrave Macmillan. 2009.

Nadel, Alan. *Flatlining on the Field of Dreams: Cultural Narratives in President Reagan's America*. New Brunswick, NJ: Rutgers University Press. 1997.

Neale, Steve, 'Action-Adventure as Hollywood Genre'. Yvonne Tasker (ed.) *Action and Adventure Cinema*. London: Routledge. 2004: 71–83.

Nowell, Richard, *Blood Money: A History of the First Teen Slasher Film Cycle*. New York: Continuum. 2011.

Paul, William. *Laughing, Screaming: Modern Hollywood Horror and Comedy*. New York: Columbia University Press. 1994.

Pomerance, Murray, 'The Man-Boys of Steven Spielberg'. Murray Pomerance and Frances Gateward (eds) *Where the Boys are: Cinemas of Masculinity and Youth*. Detroit, Michigan: Wayne State University Press. 2004. 133–54.

Pomerance, Murray, and Frances Gateward. 'Introduction'. Murray Pomerance and Frances Gateward (eds) *Where the Boys are: Cinemas of Masculinity and Youth*. Detroit, Michigan: Wayne State University Press. 2004: 1–18.

Poll, Ryan. *Main Street and Empire: The Fictional Small Town in the Age of Globalization*. New Brunswick, NJ: Rutgers University Press. 2012.

Prince, Stephen (ed.) *American Cinema of the 1980s: Themes and Variations*. New Brunswick, NJ: Rutgers University Press. 2007.

Rehling, Nichola. *Extra-ordinary Men: White Heterosexual Masculinity and Contemporary Popular Cinema*. Plymouth: Lexington Books. 2009.

Ritzer, George. *Enchanting a Disenchanted World: Continuity and Change in the Cathedrals of Consumption*. 3rd Edition. London: Pine Forge Press/SAGE Publications. 2010.

Rowley, Stephen. *Movie Towns and Sitcom Suburbs: Building Hollywood's Ideal Communities*. Basingstoke, Hampshire: Palgrave Macmillan. 2015.

Ryan, Chris. '"Stranger Things" Phones Home'. *The Ringer*. 18 July 2016. https://www.theringer.com/2016/7/18/16077074/stranger-things-netflix-80s-duffer-brothers-279deac579a9

Schauer, Bradley. *Escape Velocity: American Science Fiction Film, 1950–1982*. Middletown, CT: Wesleyan University Press. 2017.

Schober, Adrian, and Debbie C. Olson (eds). *Children in the Films of Steven Spielberg*. Plymouth, UK: Lexington Books. 2016.

Segrave, Kerry. *Product Placement in Hollywood Films: A History*. Jefferson, NC: MacFarland and Co. 2004.

Shary, Timothy. *Teen Movies: American Youth on Screen*. New York: Columbia University Press. 2006.

Sobchack, Vivian. *Screening Space: The American Science Fiction Film*. New Brunswick, NJ: Rutgers University Press. 1997.

Stephens, John (ed.) *Ways of Being Male: Representing Masculinities in Children's Literature and Film*. London: Routledge. 2002.

Strauss, William and Neil Howe, *Millennials Rising: The Next Great Generation*. New York: Vintage. 2000.

Suvin, Darko. 'Considering the Sense of "Fantasy" or "Fantastic Fiction": An Effusion', *Metamorphoses of Science Fiction: On the Poetics and History of a Literary Genre*. Ed. Gerry Canavan. Bern, Switzerland: Peter Lang. 2016: 381–444.

Vermeulen, Timotheus. *Scenes from the Suburbs: The Suburb in Contemporary US Film and Television*. Edinburgh: Edinburgh University Press. 2014.

Wallerstein, Immanuel. *Historical Capitalism with Capitalist Civilisation*. 3rd Edition. New York/London: Verso. 2011.

Walters, James. *Fantasy Film: A Critical Introduction*. Oxford: Berg. 2011.

Williams, Linda. 'Melodrama Revisited'. Nick Browne (ed.) *Refiguring American Film Genres: History and Theory*. Berkeley: University of California Press. 1998: 42–88.

Wojik-Andrews, Ian. *Children's Films: History, Ideology, Pedagogy, Theory*. New York: Routledge. 2000.

Wood, Robin. *Hollywood: From Vietnam to Reagan... And Beyond. Expanded and Revised Edition*. New York: Columbia University Press. 2003.

Zipes, Jack. *Fairy Tales and the Art of Subversion*. 2nd Edition. Oxford: Routledge. 1983 [2012].

Zipes, Jack. 'The Cultural Homogenization of American Children'. *Sticks and Stones: The Troublesome Success of Children's Literature from Slovenly Pete to Harry Potter*. London: Routledge. 2001: 1–23.

## INDEX

CPSIA information can be obtained
at www.ICGtesting.com
Printed in the USA
LVHW041927050219
606505LV00005B/7/P